THE SIN OF SODOM

THE SIN OF SODOM

WHAT THE BIBLE REALLY TEACHES ABOUT
WHY GOD DESTROYED THE CITIES OF THE PLAIN

LEE ALLEN HOWARD

Acceptable Books
Jamestown, NY

Scripture References

Scripture passages quoted are from the New Revised Standard Version, unless otherwise noted.

CEB   COMMON ENGLISH BIBLE, © 2011 by Common English Bible.

ESV   THE HOLY BIBLE, ENGLISH STANDARD VERSION, © 2001 by Crossway Bibles, a publishing ministry of Good News Publishers.

HCSB   HOLMAN CHRISTIAN STANDARD BIBLE, © 1999, 2000, 2002, 2003, 2009 by Holman Bible Publishers, Nashville Tennessee.

KJV   HOLY BIBLE, KING JAMES VERSION, 1611. Public domain.

MSG   THE MESSAGE, © 1993, 1994, 1995, 1996, 2000, 2001, 2002 by Eugene H. Peterson.

NASB   NEW AMERICAN STANDARD BIBLE, © 1960, 1962, 1963, 1968, 1971, 1972, 1973, 1975, 1977, 1995 by The Lockman Foundation.

NIV   HOLY BIBLE, NEW INTERNATIONAL VERSION®, © 1973, 1978, 1984, 2011 by Biblica, Inc.® Used by permission.

NKJV   NEW KING JAMES VERSION®, © 1982 by Thomas Nelson. Used by permission.

NLT   HOLY BIBLE. NEW LIVING TRANSLATION, © 1996, 2004, 2007, 2013 by Tyndale House Foundation. Used by permission of Tyndale House Publishers Inc., Carol Stream, Illinois 60188.

NRSV   NEW REVISED STANDARD VERSION BIBLE, © 1989 the Division of Christian Education of the National Council of the Churches of Christ in the United States of America. Used by permission.

RSV   REVISED STANDARD VERSION OF THE BIBLE, © 1946, 1952, and 1971 the Division of Christian Education of the National Council of the Churches of Christ in the United States of America. Used by permission.

When all the prisoners of the land
    are crushed under foot,
when human rights are perverted
    in the presence of the Most High,
when one's case is subverted—
    does the Lord not see it?

—*LAMENTATIONS 3:34–36*

Contents

1. Introduction

What does the Bible really teach about the sin of Sodom and its destruction with Gomorrah and surrounding cities?

Many Bible readers believe they know what the Scriptures state, yet have never closely studied the account of Sodom and Gomorrah. Others believe and promote what their church or favorite preachers proclaim without questioning these leaders' conclusions.

Serious students of the Bible would do well to develop a noble and generous character like the Bereans who, after they heard Paul preach, "received the message with great eagerness and *examined the Scriptures* every day to see if what Paul said was true" (Ac. 17:11 NIV). The Bereans were predisposed to candidly inquire, question, and discern with an open mind, just as Pilate conducted his judicial investigation of Jesus in Luke 23:14.[1]

In addition to accurately interpreting the Bible, it's crucial to understand the customs of the ancient world so that we set Scripture passages in their proper historical context. This guards against misinterpreting the text in the light of modern traditions, beliefs, and prejudices.

---

1   See also Acts 4:9; 28:18; 1 Corinthians 2:14.

In this book we'll examine *all* the Scripture passages that mention Sodom to find out what they do—and don't—say about why God destroyed the ancient cities of the Plain. We'll also take a look at history and the interpretations of Old Testament scholars and early Church leaders to discover the way their understanding evolved over the centuries and how this affects the beliefs of today's Church.

Traditional opinion about God's destruction of Sodom

According to priest and psychotherapist John McNeill, for centuries "the Church taught, and people have universally believed… that homosexual practices had brought a terrible divine vengeance on the cities of Sodom and Gomorrah" (McNeill 42). Stated simply, many Christians believe God rained down fire and brimstone on the cities because its inhabitants were gay.

The medieval Church believed that when homosexual activity increased in their day, it brought God's wrath on their communities. About A.D. 1220, Paul of Hungary wrote in his *Summa of Penance,* "The [Church] law says that because of this crime there come about famine and plagues, and earth-quakes." Therefore, they needed to ward off God's judgment by rooting out and punishing any homosexuals in their midst (McNeill 42).

This idea still persists today. Pat Robertson agreed with the late Jerry Falwell that the September 9, 2011, terrorist attacks on the U.S. were caused by "pagans, abortionists, feminists, gays, lesbians, the American Civil Liberties Union and the People For the American Way" (Pat Robertson Controversies).

Much of the conservative Church still believes the sin that resulted in the destruction of those ancient cities was "the habitual indulgence of perverse homosexual practices among men" (McNeill 42).

But, outside of the Genesis account of Sodom, is there any evidence elsewhere in the Bible to support that homosexual behavior was prevalent in these cities?

What does the Bible really teach about Sodom?

We'll start by looking at two chapters in Genesis.

Preparing for the study

I invite you to read carefully chapters 18 and 19 of Genesis. These two chapters are reproduced in "Appendix A: Genesis 18–19 NRSV" on page 163. You also may want to read chapters 11 through 17, but 18 and 19 are crucial to our study.

To discover what the Bible really says about the destruction of the ancient cities of the Plain, we must preface our analysis with background that sets the stage and introduces the players. Let's begin with Abram and Lot.

2. Abram and Lot Move to Canaan

About 3800 years ago in the land of Mesopotamia lived a man named Terah, a descendant of Noah through Shem. He dwelt in Ur, "an important Sumerian city-state in ancient Mesopotamia, located at the site of modern Tell el-Muqayyar in south Iraq's Dhi Qar Governorate" (Ur).

Terah's family in Ur

When Terah was seventy years old, he fathered Abram, Nahor, and Haran (Gen. 11:26). He also had a daughter Sarai by a different wife. Therefore, Sarai was Abram's half-sister (20:12).

Haran's wife is not named, but he had a son named Lot and a daughter named Milcah. Haran died relatively young, before his father and brothers.

Nahor married his niece Milcah, and Abram married Sarai, who was barren (11:28-30). Josephus the Jewish historian mentions that Abram adopted Lot because Haran had died and Abram had no son of his own (Josephus Antiq. 1.7.1).

Centuries later, Joshua son of Nun told the tribes of Israel gathered at Shechem, "Thus says the Lord, the God of Israel: Long ago your ancestors—Terah and his sons Abraham and Nahor—lived beyond the Euphrates and served other gods. Then I took your father Abraham from beyond the River and led him through all the land of Canaan" (Josh. 24:2-3).

Ur Kasdim is identified with the Sumerian city of Ur, where the Chaldeans settled much later, around the ninth century B.C. Ur was the sacred city of the moon god.[2] "Abraham's ancestors may have been moon-worshippers, an idea based on the possibility that the name of Abraham's father Terah is related to the Hebrew root for moon (*y-r-h*)" (Ur Kasdim).

God called Abram in Ur

Moments before Stephen was martyred, he spoke to the Sanhedrin about Abraham:

> [2]"Brothers and fathers," he said, "listen: The God of glory appeared to our father Abraham *when he was in Mesopotamia, before he settled in Haran,* [3]and said to him: Get out of your country and away from your relatives, and come to the land that I will show you. [4]Then he came out of the land of the Chaldeans and settled in Haran. From there, after his father died, God had him move to this land you now live in."
>
> —*ACTS 7:2-4 HCSB*

God originally spoke to Abram and called him while he still lived in Ur. Genesis 12:1 says, "The Lord had said to Abram, 'Go from your country, your people and your father's household to the land I will show you" (NIV).

---

2   "Sin (Akkadian) or Nanna (Sumerian) was the god of the moon in the Mesopotamian mythology of Akkad, Assyria and Babylonia. Nanna is a Sumerian deity, the son of Enlil and Ninlil, and became identified with Semitic Sin. The two chief seats of Nanna's/Sin's worship were Ur in the south of Mesopotamia and Harran in the north. The main shrine to Nanna was the Ziggurat of Ur. Nanna's chief sanctuary at Ur was named E-gish-shir-gal ("house of the great light"). (Sin)

But it was Terah who took Abram, Sarai, and his grandson Lot and left Ur, settling in Haran (Gen. 11:31). "Haran was in northeast Mesopotamia on the river Belias, about sixty miles above its confluence with the Euphrates. It was a trade center on the route from Ninevah to Carchemish (Ezek. 27:23)" (Dake).

Terah died in the city of Haran at the age of 205 (Gen. 11:32).

God speaks to Abram again

God apparently spoke to Abram again at age seventy-five and told him to leave his father's house and go to Canaan. There, God would make of him "a great nation" (12:1–2), meaning Abram would have many descendants.

Abram and Sarai left, and Lot went with them, taking all their possessions and the people they had acquired in Haran, finally arriving at Canaan (12:4–5).

At Shechem[3], "the Lord appeared to Abram, and said, 'To your offspring I will give this land.' So he built there an altar to the Lord, who had appeared to him." Abram then moved on to the hill country east of Bethel[4], journeying "by stages toward the Negeb[5]" (12:7–8).

---

3   Shechem is about fifteen miles west of the Jordan River, very close to Mt. Gerazim, which was later referred to as the hill country of Israel (May 57).

4   Twenty miles south of Shechem, near Ai (May 57).

5   The Negeb is a broad area that lies between the Great Sea (Mediterranean) and the fertile Valley of Siddim, which extends southernward beyond the bottom end of the Salt Sea (May 57).

After a side trip to Egypt (12:10–20), they finally settled at Bethel with all their flocks and herds (13:1–4). But a problem developed there.

3. Abram and Lot Separate

Abram and Lot grew so prosperous they had to part ways because there was not enough room for all their tents and insufficient grazing land for both of their herds and flocks, which had grown quite large (Gen. 13:5-6). Because of this overcrowding, "there was strife between the herders of Abram's livestock and the herders of Lot's livestock" (13:7).

Abram graciously let Lot choose where to settle, and Lot looked toward the plain.

> [10]Lot looked about him, and saw that the plain of the Jordan was well watered everywhere like the garden of the Lord, like the land of Egypt, in the direction of Zoar; this was before the Lord had destroyed Sodom and Gomorrah. [11]So Lot chose for himself all the plain of the Jordan, and Lot journeyed eastwards; thus they separated from each other. [12]Abram settled in the land of Canaan, while *Lot settled among the cities of the Plain and moved his tent as far as Sodom.*
> —GENESIS 13:10-12

Sodom was one of five small cities, including Gomorrah, Admah, Zeboim, and Bela (or Zoar), called "the cities of the Plain" (13:12 KJV). These cities lay situated on the plain of the Jordan River in an area along the southern limit of the lands of the Canaanite people—good grazing land.

Abram remained in Canaan, settling by the oak (terebinth) grove of Mamre (13:18), an Amorite who owned much property. In time, Abraham entered into an alliance with Mamre and his brothers Eshcol and Aner. "The relationship seems to have been mutually beneficial—use of the land in exchange for military support" (Harris, Archer and Waltke, 1208).

The land of Mamre is "about two miles north of Hebron" (1208) and seventeen miles west of the Salt Sea—the Sea of Arabah, later known as the Dead Sea (Oxford 57).

Lot chose the plain of the Jordan because it was lush. He pitched his tent *"toward Sodom"* (KJV), yet outside the city.

Topology of the Plain

The geographical topology of the Dead Sea area in that time was different from what it is today. The sea was smaller at its southern end, and the Plain, extending south of the Valley of Siddim, was dry but fertile land. It is now covered with water, as shown in the following map. Possible locations of Sodom, Gomorrah, and Zoar are indicated.

Genesis 19:28 says that Abraham "looked down" from Hebron and saw the destruction of the cities of the Plain. The mention of bitumen pits (Gen. 14:10) indicates the cities were south of the Dead Sea (at its size then) because bitumen, a petroleum product similar to asphalt, "was commonly found in the shallow southern basin of the Dead Sea in antiquity" (Wood).[6]

Josephus indicates that Sodom was near the Dead Sea, which he refers to by its Greek name, Asphaltites. He also mentions "slime pits" in the area. (Josephus Antiq. 1.9)

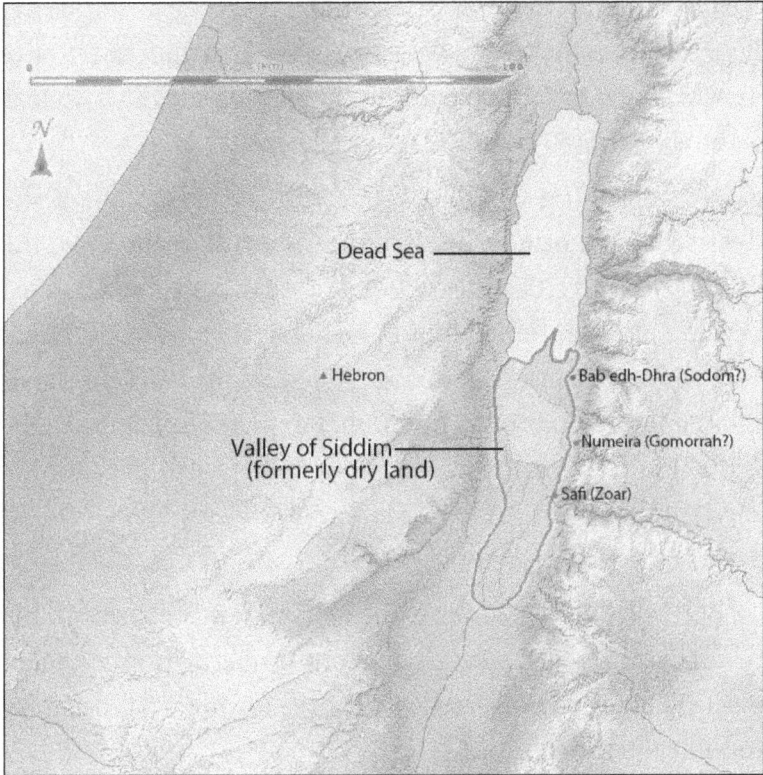

Dead Sea

Hebron

Valley of Siddim
(formerly dry land)

Bab edh-Dhra (Sodom?)

Numeira (Gomorrah?)

Safi (Zoar)

Possible location of the cities

The only towns known to be inhabited in the Dead Sea region between 3300 and 900 B.C. are Bab edh-Dhra and Numeira. Bab edh-Dhra is the largest of the two and is identified with Sodom; Numeira with Gomorrah[7].[8]

---

6   The Summer 1999 issue of *Bible and Spade*, the magazine of the Associates for Biblical Research, which is committed to using archaeology to demonstrate the historical veracity of the Old and New Testaments, included a lengthy and detailed article by Bryant G. Wood concerning the location of the cities of Sodom and Gomorrah that will be referenced in coming pages.

The ancient Greek historian Strabo reveals that "locals living near Moasada (as opposed to Masada) say that 'there were once thirteen inhabited cities in that region of which Sodom was the metropolis'" (Sodom: Wikipedia).

Not wanting to flee to the mountains during the destruction, Lot and his daughters headed for Zoar, the smallest of the cities (Gen. 19:17–23). Zoar continued to exist because it is mentioned in prophecies against Moab in Isaiah 15:5 and Jeremiah 48:34. It is identified on the Madaba map, a mosaic in the floor of a church that depicted Palestine in the sixth century. The town is located on the southeast shore of the Dead Sea, just south of the Zared River, placing ancient Zoar in the vicinity of modern Safi (Wood).

Bab edh-Dhra/Sodom is the "largest ancient ruin in the region.... It was occupied throughout the Early Bronze Age for a period of over 1,000 years." Numeira, however, was occupied for only a century. (Wood)

---

7   "The consonants of the name Gomorrah are *c (ayin) MR* and the consonants of Numeira are *N M R*. The ancient and modern names match, except for the first letter. Initial laryngeals like the *ayin* in *cMR* were commonly lost or transformed in the process of time, or when they came over into other languages or dialects. In this case, it is possible that nasalization took place, so the *ayin* in Hebrew *cMR* became the *N* in Arabic *NMR*" (Wood).

8   "Possible candidates for Sodom or Gomorrah are the sites discovered or visited by Walter E. Rast and R. Thomas Schaub in 1973, including Bab edh-Dhra, which was originally excavated in 1965 by archaeologist Paul Lapp, and later finished by Rast and Schaub following his death. Other possibilities also include Numeira, al-Safi, Feifa and Khanazir, which were also visited by Schaub and Rast. All sites were located near the Dead Sea, with evidence of burning and traces of sulfur" (Sodom: Wikipedia).

In 1975 a great archive of clay tablets dating to 2400–2350 B.C. was discovered at Tell Mardikh, ancient Ebla, in northern Syria (Archi 1997). One of the tablets is a geographic atlas listing 289 place names. … In the area corresponding to the east side of the Dead Sea Plain there are two places named— Number 210, Admah, and Number 211, Sodom. If Shea's readings are correct, this would be the only confirmed mention of the Cities of the Plain outside the Bible. But why were not the other three cities, Gomorrah, Zoar, and Zeboiim, mentioned? The excavations at Numeira perhaps can shed some light on that question. These excavations revealed that Numeira (= Gomorrah) was in existence for only a short period of time, less than 100 years. It appears that the Ebla Atlas was composed prior to the founding of Numeira. The same may true of Zoar and Zeboiim. (Wood)

The etymology of the name Numeira is uncertain but could be based on the root *gh m r*, which means "be deep," "copious water" (Sodom: Wikipedia). Numeira is situated at 920–950 feet below sea level, earning it the designation as the world's lowest city (Wood).

Agriculture in the Plain

During the Early Bronze Age, the level of the Dead Sea was at a low point. Thus, "the shallow basin, or 'plain' south of the Dead Sea, would have been dry land and probably cultivated." The cities of the Plain "had a close association, or connection, with the plain" and "were doubtless dependent upon the plain for their livelihood. (Wood)

Genesis 13:10 says that the Plain was "well watered," *mashqeh* in Hebrew (Strong's H4945), meaning "cupbearer, drink"

(Wood)

(Harris, Archer and Waltke, 2452c). It was lush like the "garden of the Lord," areas well-irrigated for agricultural fruitfulness (see Isa. 58:11). Wood states that agriculture was important to the economic base of these cities in this region and that irrigation was key to their industry.

Lot chose the well-watered land of the Plain to raise his herds. And he moved very close to Sodom.

The people of Sodom

Genesis 13:13 states, "Now the *people* of Sodom were wicked, great sinners against the Lord." The word *people* is *enôsh* in Hebrew, meaning "mortals," and is not the same word typically used for "man" (*'adam*) (Strong's H582).

The basic meaning of *enôsh* is "man" in the sense of "mankind." ... If it is a derivation of *anash*, "to be weak, sick," the basic emphasis would be on man's weakness or mortality (Harris, Archer and Waltke, 582).

We see that all the people of Sodom—not just the men—were criminally sinful. The use of *enôsh* here points up their weakness and mortality, as if their days are numbered.

4. Lot Becomes a Prisoner of War

During the ten-year time span between Abram and Lot separating and Ishmael being born, trouble developed among the cities of the Plain and the kingdom of Elam.

Rebellion against Elamite rule

At that time, King Bera[9] ruled Sodom, and King Birsha[10] ruled Gomorrah. "Their kingship, however, was not sovereign, because all of the river Jordan plain was under Elamite rule for twelve years. The kingdom of Elam was ruled by King Chedorlaomer[11] [Genesis 14:1–4]" (Sodom: Wikipedia).

The Elamite civilization began east of the Tigris and Euphrates plains. What was the strong suit of this kingdom?

> Elamite strength was based on an ability to hold these various areas together under a coordinated government that permitted the maximum interchange of the natural resources unique to each region. Traditionally, this was done through a federated governmental structure (Elam: Wikipedia).

---

9 *Bera* means "gift" (Packer, Tenney and White 615).

10 *Birsha* means "thick, strong" (Packer, Tenney and White 617).

11 *Chedorlaomer*, or Kutir-Lakamar, means "servant of the goddess Lakamar" (Packer, Tenney and White 618). *Lakamar* means "no mercy."

If this was the strength of Elamite rule, the fertile plain surrounding the Dead Sea would have been a cradle of wealth and natural resources for them, and subject to competition among local rulers. The Bible picks up the story:

> [1]In the days of King Amraphel of Shinar[12], King Arioch of Ellasar, King Chedorlaomer of Elam, and King Tidal of Goiim[13], [2]these kings made war with King Bera of Sodom, King Birsha of Gomorrah, King Shinab of Admah[14], King Shemeber of Zeboiim[15], and the king of Bela (that is, Zoar[16]). [3]All these joined forces in the Valley of Siddim (that is, the Dead Sea). [4]Twelve years they had served Chedorlaomer, but *in the thirteenth year they rebelled.*
> —*GENESIS 14:1–4*

This tells us ultimately of the conflict between Chedorlaomer and his loyal vassals with the rebellious kings of the cities of the Plain. But their battle was preceded by a military

---

12 Shinar, also called Akkad, was a plain in southwestern Mesopotamia, later known as Babylonia. "In Genesis 10:10 we are told that the great tyrant and empire builder Nimrod founded his kingdom in Babel, Erech (Sumerian Uruk), Akkad (Agade) and Calneh in the land of Shinar. From here he pushed north into Assyria. It was here also, in Shinar, that rebellious man built the well-known tower of Babel in direct defiance of God (Genesis 11:2)" (Harris, Archer and Waltke, 2424).

13 *Goiim* means "nations," but "Bible commentaries suggest that that in this verse it may instead be a reference to the region of Gutium" (Tidal). The Gutians "were a tribe from northern and central ranges of the Zagros Mountains that overran southern Mesopotamia when the Akkadian empire collapsed in approximately 2154 BC. Sumerian sources portray the Gutians as a barbarous, ravenous people" (Gutian).

14 *Admah* is a contraction of *'adamah*, meaning "earthy" (Strong's H126).

15 *Zeboiim* (plural) means "gazelles, roes" (Easton).

16 *Zoar* means "'small' or 'insignificance' in Hebrew" (Zoara).

campaign against a number of other nations in the land of Canaan.

> [5]In the fourteenth year Chedorlaomer and the kings who were with him[17] came and subdued the Rephaim in Ashteroth-karnaim, the Zuzim in Ham, the Emim in Shaveh-kiriathaim, [6]and the Horites in the hill country of Seir as far as El-paran on the edge of the wilderness; [7]then they turned back and came to En-mishpat (that is, Kadesh), and *subdued* all the country of the Amalekites, and also the Amorites who lived in Hazazon-tamar.
>
> —GENESIS 14:5–7

Chedorlaomer's great war

Subdued means "to strike, slay, destroy" (Strong's H5221). Chedorlaomer and allies apparently spent an entire year in war against the peoples listed. For more information about them, see "Appendix B: Peoples of Genesis 14:5–7" on page 169.

Chedorlaomer's military campaign was quite broad-ranging, traversing hundreds of miles, covering the entire land of Canaan east of the Sea of Chinnereth, the Jordan River, and the Salt Sea, all the way down to the Sinai Peninsula. Perhaps one of Chedorlaomer's goals was "to clear the caravan route to the Red Sea" (Harris, Archer and Waltke, 1728).

Chedorlaomer and allies fight against the cities of the Plain

Toward the end of this war, Chedorlaomer and his allies faced off with the rebellious kings of the cities of the Plain.

---

17 Amraphel, Arioch, and Tidal.

⁸Then the king of Sodom, the king of Gomorrah, the king of
Admah, the king of Zeboiim, and the king of Bela (that is,
Zoar) went out, and they joined battle in the Valley of Siddim
⁹with King Chedorlaomer of Elam, King Tidal of Goiim,
King Amraphel of Shinar, and King Arioch of Ellasar, four
kings against five.
—*GENESIS 14:8–9*

Here are the allies and opponents:

Elamite Allies	Opponents from Cities of the Plain
Chedorlaomer of Elam	Bera of Sodom
Tidal of Goiim	Birsha of Gomorrah
Amraphel of Shinar	Shinab of Admah
Arioch of Ellasar	Shemeber of Zeboiim
	Unnamed king of Bela/Zoar

The year following the rebellion, Chedorlaomer mustered his
forces with three of the kings loyal to Elamite rule—
Amraphel[18], Arioch[19], Tidal[20]—and marched forth to suppress

---

18 *Amraphel* means "powerful people" (609). "Thought to be Hammurabi,
    king of Babylon, who was a celebrated warrior, builder, and lawgiver of
    the famous Babylonian Code of Laws regulating courts of justice and
    daily life of his subjects" (Dake).

19 *Arioch* means "lion-like" (Packer, Tenney and White 610). The same as
    Eri-Aku of Larsa. "Eri-Aku's inscriptions inform us that Ur (Muqayyari,
    Mugheir) was in the principality of which Larsa was the capital" (Bible
    Names).

20 *Tidal* means "fearfulness" (Strong's H8413).

the rebellion of five kings of the cities of the Plain: Bera, Birsha, Shinab[21], Shemeber[22], and the king of Bela/Zoar.

They mobilized for war in the Valley of Siddim, meaning "the tilled field" (Packer, Tenney and White 727). *Smith's Bible Dictionary* tells us:

> This term [*emeq*, meaning "valley" (Strong's H6010)] appears to have been assigned to a broad, flattish tract, sometimes of considerable width, enclosed on each side by a definite range of hills. It has so far a suitable spot for the combat between the four and five kings, verse 8; but it contained a multitude of bitumen-pits sufficient materially to affect the issue of the battle. In this valley the kings of the five allied cities of Sodom, Gomorrah, Admah, Zeboim and Bela seem to have awaited the approach of the invaders. (Smith "Siddim")

Success remained with Chedorlaomer and his vassals during this battle in the Valley of Siddim.

> ¹⁰Now the Valley of Siddim was full of *bitumen pits*; and as the kings of Sodom and Gomorrah fled, some fell into them, and the rest fled to the hill country. ¹¹So the enemy took all the goods of Sodom and Gomorrah, and all their provisions, and went their way; ¹²they also took Lot, the son of Abram's brother, who lived in Sodom, and his goods, and departed.
> —*GENESIS 14:10–12*

Chedorlaomer and allies routed the armies of the five rebellious kings, who finally fled in retreat. *Fled* (*nûs*) "denotes

---

21 *Shinab* means "a father has turned" (Strong's H8134).

22 *Shemeber* means "name of pinion (illustrious)" (Strong's H8038); "soaring on high," "lofty flight," "name of force" (Bible Names).

rapid movement away from something or someone… It usually connotes escape from real or imagined danger…, the basic
image being martial (cf. Leviticus 26:36)" (Harris, Archer and
Waltke, 1327). As they fled, they *fell* (*napal*), where "a violent or
accidental circumstance is often indicated" (Harris, Archer and
Waltke, 1392).

Bitumen pits, or *slimepits* in the KJV, is the Hebrew word
be'er, which in addition to designating slime or bitumen pits,
indicates a place of destruction (Psalm 55:23; Psalm 69:15)"
(Harris, Archer and Waltke, 194e).

Was it poor defense or bad luck at play here? Considering
Chedorlaomer's success in the previous year against mighty
Canaanite armies that consisted of the giant Rephaim and
related tribes[23], perhaps God was with the four kings to subdue
Sodom's contingent. Those who survived the attack fled to the
surrounding mountains, leaving their home cities unpro-
tected.

Chedorlaomer collects the spoils of war

Genesis 14:13 says that Chedorlaomer's army "took all the
goods of Sodom and Gomorrah, and all their provisions."
They seized the *goods* (*rekûsh*):

> It covers a wide variety of property including: movable
> possessions of all kinds (Genesis 14:16, 21); cattle and other
> domestic animals (Genesis 31:18); movable property besides
> cattle (Genesis 46:6); supplies and stores (Daniel 11:13, KJV,
> "much riches," RSV "abundant supplies").… One special
> meaning is the "spoil" or "booty" of war (2 Chron. 20:25;

---

23 See "Appendix B: Peoples of Genesis 14:5–7" on page 169.

2 Chron. 21:14, 17; Daniel 11:24, 28.) (Harris, Archer and Waltke, 2167b)

They also took the *provisions*, meaning food (Strong's H400). The conquerors sacked the five cities of their material possessions and food supplies. This was no small feat.

The name *Sodom* could be related to the Arabic *sadama*, meaning "fasten, fortify, strengthen" (Sodom: Wikipedia). Both Sodom (Bab edh-Dhra) and Gomorrah (Numeira) were fortified cities with walls and gates.

Chedorlaomer's forces probably destroyed the west gate and entered the city that way. The Associates for Biblical Research (biblearchaeology.org) published a fascinating article about the archaeology of what is believed to be Sodom. Bryant Wood explains:

> About 25 years before the final destruction, however, Bab edh-Dhra [Sodom] suffered a destruction which caused the citizens to purposely block up the west gate and construct a new gate on the northeast. This can be linked to the attack of the coalition of Mesopotamian kings described in Genesis 14.

Wood says that for most of the history of Bab edh-Dhra, the city's main entrance was located on the west side, providing access to the plain below. Within its last 100 years of occupation, however, the west wall and gate suffered a major destruction, resulting in the citizens intentionally blocking the west gate and building a new gate in the northeast. The new gate was built atop a meter of burned debris left from the calamity (Wood).

Excavations revealed stone-lined grain storage pits at Gomorrah/Numeira. Such underground structures were used to store foodstuffs in the cities of the Plain, and these were likely robbed during the pillaging of Sodom.

The conquering kings also took captive the *people* of the cities, for in 14:21, King Bera of Sodom asks for the return of the "persons"—*nephesh*, meaning breathing, living souls (Strong's H5315). Among the people abducted was Abram's nephew Lot along with all his goods, which we know were numerous (13:5–6).

What happened next?

An escapee alerts Abram

¹³Then one who had escaped came and told Abram the Hebrew, who was living by the oaks of Mamre the Amorite, brother of Eshcol and of Aner; these were allies of Abram. ¹⁴When Abram heard that his nephew had been taken captive, he led forth his trained men, born in his house, three hundred eighteen of them, and went in pursuit as far as Dan.
—*GENESIS 14:13–14*

Someone escaped either the battle (14:10) or the sacking of the cities, and this one apparently knew Lot had an uncle, "Abram the Hebrew." The first biblical occurrence of the word *Hebrew* is in verse 13, "from `eber (H5676), meaning 'across,' or 'the opposite side'" (Dake, Gen. 14:13).

The fugitive told Abram that Lot had been taken *captive*: "In the OT *shabâ* chiefly conveys the idea of a military or para-military force subduing a foe and then taking into their possession the men, women, children, cattle, and wealth of the defeated party" (Harris, Archer and Waltke, 2311).

Abram gives chase and battles

Abram left Mamre, west of the Salt Sea, with 318 trained men from his own household. His Amorite allies, Aner, Eshcol, and Mamre, went with him (14:24). They pursued the conquering kings "as far as Dan."

Although the territory did not yet belong to the tribe of Dan, it was the northernmost area of Canaan, above the Sea of Chinnereth, about *165 miles* (as the crow flies) from the Valley of Siddim.

Considering that Chedorlaomer defeated powerful nations during his war campaign the previous year, it is likely that Abram's forces were vastly outnumbered. What did Abram the man of faith do?

> [15]He divided his forces against them by night, he and his servants, and routed them and pursued them to Hobah, north of Damascus. [16]Then he brought back all the goods, and also brought back his nephew Lot with his goods, and the women and the *people.*
>
> —*GENESIS 14:15–16*

With Abram's elite force (trained servants!), they routed the enemy, chasing them to Hobah, a place "sixty miles north-west of Damascus" (Dake, Gen. 14:15). He brought back all the goods, Lot and his possessions, and *all the people*—men, women, and children. People here is *am*, meaning "people as a congregated unit" (Strong's H5971).

With so many people and possessions, it must have taken them weeks to return to Shaveh-kiriathaim, west of the Salt Sea—about 180 miles.

¹⁷After [Abram's] return from the defeat of Chedorlaomer and the kings who were with him, the king of Sodom went out to meet him at the Valley of Shaveh (that is, the King's Valley). ¹⁸And King Melchizedek of Salem brought out bread and wine; he was priest of God Most High. ¹⁹He blessed him and said,

"Blessed be Abram by God Most High,
  maker of heaven and earth;
²⁰and blessed be God Most High,
  who has delivered your enemies into your hand!"
And Abram gave him one-tenth of everything.
—*GENESIS 14:17–20*

After Abram and his little army of servants defeated the kings and rescued the goods and people that had been captured from the cities of the Plain, two kings approached him in the Valley of Shaveh: Bera, the king of Sodom, and the king and priest of Salem, Melchizedek, who had taken no part in the war.

Melchizedek means "king of righteousness," and *Salem* means "peace." Salem later became Jerusalem, just northwest of the Salt Sea. "Melchizedek was a Gentile whose priesthood is eternal in Christ (Ps. 110:4; Heb. 5:10; 6:20; 7:1–28)." Here also is the first mention of the word *priest*. (Dake, Gen. 14:18)

Bera brought Abram nothing, showing no hospitality. But Melchizedek brought bread and wine as gestures of friendship and goodwill, and he blessed Abram, acknowledging that El-Elyon had delivered his enemies into his hand. Abram gave him one-tenth of the spoils of war.

For more information about the doctrine of tithing, see my book, *The Truth About Tithing: What the Bible Really Teaches* (Lee A. Howard, 2013).

Abram sets free the people of Sodom

> Then the king of Sodom said to Abram, "Give me the
> persons, but take the goods for yourself."
> —*GENESIS 14:21*

King Bera negotiated with Abram about what had been
recovered from Chedorlaomer. He said, "Keep the booty, but
give me the people"—the *nephesh*, the souls.

Since Abram had defeated Chedorlaomer's forces and won
the spoils of war, by right he could keep everything he had
captured.

> [22]But Abram said to the king of Sodom, "I have sworn to the
> Lord, God Most High, maker of heaven and earth, [23]that I
> would not take a thread or a sandal-thong or anything that is
> yours, so that you might not say, 'I have made Abram rich.'
> [24]I will take nothing but what the young men have eaten, and
> the share of the men who went with me—Aner, Eshcol, and
> Mamre. Let them take their share."
> —*GENESIS 14:22-24*

Abram's Source was God alone, and he refused to take anything from King Bera, providing only for his allies. He gave the
rest to Bera, and Lot went free, returning to Sodom.

5. Abraham's Divine Visitation

After Abram returned from meeting with Melchizedek and Bera in the Valley of Shaveh, God entered covenant with him (Gen. 15), and Ishmael was conceived and born of Hagar (Gen. 16).

> [1]When Abram was ninety-nine years old, the Lord appeared to Abram, and said to him, "I am God Almighty; walk before me, and be blameless. [2]And I will make my covenant between me and you, and will make you exceedingly numerous."
> —Genesis 17:1–2

The all-powerful El Shaddai renewed covenant with Abram, changing his name to *Abraham*, "father of a multitude" (Strong's H85), and giving him the sign of circumcision (Gen. 17:5, 10–14, 23–27). God also changed Sarai's name to *Sarah*, "mother of princes" (Dake, Gen. 17:15).

Time of the destruction

We now must plot the time of the events from Genesis 14–19.

The account of the Elamite war falls between the time Abraham left Haran when he was 75 (12:4) and the conception of Ishmael when Abraham was 85 (16:3). Because Sodom and Gomorrah were destroyed near the conception of Isaac when Abraham was 99 (17:1; 21:5), the attack on Sodom and

Gomorrah by the Mesopotamian kings took place between 14 and 24 years before the final fiery holocaust.

> Since the Lord told Abraham and Sarah about the coming birth of Isaac just prior to the destruction (Gn 18:10–14), the date of the destruction can be calculated based on the birth date of Isaac. If we assume a mid-15th century B.C. date for the Exodus, the date for the destruction would then be ca. 2070 B.C. (Wood)

When the angels visited Abraham, the Lord announced, "At the appointed time I will return to you, in the *spring*, and Sarah shall have a son" (Gen. 18:14 RSV). This would place the angelic visit and the destruction of the Plain cities in late spring or early summer.

Whole, carbonized grapes were found at the excavation of Gomorrah/Numeira in 1977 and 1981. This reveals the time of year the cities were destroyed. "The fact that the grapes were intact," says Wood, "indicates that they were freshly harvested. In the hot climate of the Dead Sea valley the harvesting of grapes occurs earlier than other parts of the country—in the late spring or early summer" (Wood).

Three visitors appear

Let's pick up the story proper in Genesis 18.

> [1]The Lord appeared to Abraham by the oaks of Mamre, as he sat at the entrance of his tent in the heat of the day. [2]He looked up and saw three men standing near him. When he saw them, he ran from the tent entrance to meet them, and bowed down to the ground.
>
> —*GENESIS 18:1-2*

The account begins by saying that the *Lord* appeared to Abraham. He is the central character. The traditional interpretation of the appearance of the three visitors is that one is the Lord appearing in human form (called a *theophany*), and the other two men are angels. In any case, they are distinguished yet mysterious characters.

Abraham was sitting at the entrance of his tent in the heat of the day. With the sun beating down, the tent was very warm. He was likely sitting in the shade of the canopy over the opening. The Jamieson-Fausset-Brown *Commentary* explains that desert travelers "start at sunrise and continue till midday when they look out for some resting-place" (Gen. 18:2).

Note that Abraham *ran* to meet them.

> When the visitor is an ordinary person, the host merely rises; but if of superior rank, the custom is to advance a little towards the stranger, and after a very low bow, turn and lead him to the tent, putting an arm round his waist, or tapping him on the shoulder as they go, to assure him of welcome (Jamieson, Fausset and Brown Gen. 18:2).

It seems that Abraham had some kind of sense, whether by sight or revelation, that these visitors were very important. He rose and ran to meet them, bowing low to the ground.

Abraham's treatment of the sojourners

[3]He said, "My lord, if I find favor with you, do not pass by your servant. [4]Let a little water be brought, and wash your feet, and rest yourselves under the tree. [5]Let me bring a little bread, that you may refresh yourselves, and after that you

may pass on—since you have come to your servant." So they said, "Do as you have said."
—*GENESIS 18:3–5*

The last part of verse 5 says, "This is why you have passed your servant's way" (HCSB). Although the visitors have revealed nothing concerning their visit, "Abraham knew their object by the course they took—approaching directly in front of the chief sheik's tent, which is always distinguishable… thus showing their wish to be his guests" (Jamieson, Fausset and Brown Gen. 18:5).

In addition to his great deference, Abraham offers them what should be given to any desert sojourner: water to wash their feet and something to eat to refresh them. They acquiesce to his request. But what he actually provides is much greater than promised.

> ⁶And Abraham hastened into the tent to Sarah, and said, "Make ready quickly three measures of choice flour, knead it, and make cakes." ⁷Abraham ran to the herd, and took a calf, tender and good, and gave it to the servant, who hastened to prepare it. ⁸Then he took curds and milk and the calf that he had prepared, and set it before them; and he stood by them under the tree while they ate.
> —*GENESIS 18:6–8*

Abraham calls one of the visitors "my lord" and refers to himself as "your servant," acting as if they would be doing him a favor if they let him serve them.

He has water brought to wash their feet and then prepares a lavish meal for them. Three seahs of flour is about twenty quarts—a lot of bread for three men! He selects a choice, tender calf and has his servant prepare it. Abraham himself then brings the cooked beef as well as curds and milk. He refrains from eating but stands nearby, taking the posture of a servant (NIVSB).

Although Abraham is a powerful, wealthy man in charge of many important affairs, he runs, bows, and show his visitors lavish Near Eastern HOSPITALITY.

The importance of hospitality

The elaborate and generous hospitality of the Near and Middle East is known the world over, according to the Rev. Paul-Gordon Chandler: "For the guest, nothing is too good and nothing too bothersome or difficult" (Chandler). As John Calvin commented, this is "the hospitality of the holy man" (Calvin).

The sacred right of hospitality is called *theoxeny*, where gods disguise themselves or dispatch beggars or travelers to test human piety by requiring the hospitality. Such stories "are a commonplace of folklore in many cultures" and occur in the Bible with the Sodom and Gibeah accounts and in Deuteronomy 23:3–4. Those citizens who fail the test are punished, often violently. The uprightly hospitable, though, are rewarded with a gift or prophecy. (Boswell 96) Chandler states,

"The guest is a guest of God" is a well-known Arab Muslim proverb that reflects the theological depth of their view of hospitality. … Their model being Abraham, the patriarch, who welcomed the three mysterious strangers who came to him in the desert. For as in Abraham's experience, *in*

welcoming the stranger, we are welcoming God among us.
(Chandler, emphasis mine)

Hebrews 13:2 admonishes us, "Do not neglect to *show hospitality* to *strangers*, for by doing that some have entertained angels without knowing it." It specifically says *strangers*—not family or relatives or friends or other believers.

The Bible tells us to show hospitality to STRANGERS.

The concept to clinch before we progress in our study is that ancient Near Easterners practiced a *sacred code of hospitality that honored guests like divine dignitaries*, providing for their every need and protecting them at any cost.

As Hebrews 13:2 indicates, Abraham did in fact entertain divine messengers, for in Genesis 18:9–15, one of them promises Abraham that his barren wife Sarah—now far past menopause at age 90—will bear him a son, the start of a nation of descendants.

When the visitors finish their feast, they discuss business with Abraham.

The Lord reveals His purpose for the visit

Two of the three visitors start the journey toward Sodom, but one remains behind.

> [16]Then the men set out from there, and they looked towards Sodom; and Abraham went with them to set them on their way. [17]The Lord said, "Shall I hide from Abraham what I am about to do, [18]seeing that Abraham shall become a great and mighty nation, and all the nations of the earth shall be

blessed in him? [19]No, for I have chosen him, that he may charge his children and his household after him to *keep the way of the Lord by doing righteousness and justice*; so that the Lord may bring about for Abraham what he has promised him."
—GENESIS 18:16-19

The leader, referred to as "the Lord," decides to reveal his plans[24] to Abraham since he will become the progenitor of a "great and mighty nation" and the source of blessing for all peoples. (Romans 4:16 calls him the father of the Judeo-Christian faith. See also Galatians 3:6–14.)

Verse 19 points out why God chose Abraham to be this source of blessing: so that he would instruct his household and descendants to keep the ways of the Lord by *doing righteousness and justice.*

To ensure that we are able to receive what God promises, we also must promote righteousness and justice. "No good thing does the Lord withhold from those who walk uprightly" (Ps. 84:11b).

The blessings of God—prosperity, growth, and expansion—are for a people who promote righteousness and justice for everyone else, especially strangers.[25]

---

24 See Psalm 84:11; Amos 3:7; John 15:15; James 2:23.

25 For further study about strangers, see 1 Chronicles 29:15; Job 29:16, 31:32; Matthew 25:35.

What have we learned so far?

Establishing context is crucial to further study about Sodom and Gomorrah. In Genesis 18, we've marked the following:

- The importance of *hospitality to strangers*
- The requirement of doing *righteousness* and *justice* to ensure the blessing of a family, nation, city, or any group of people

Before we progress, let's define some terms.

What is hospitality?

Webster defines *hospitality* as "Reception and entertainment of strangers or guests without reward, or with kind and generous liberality."[26] We see theis in Abraham's treatment of his divine visitors.

What is righteousness?

Righteousness is being in right relationship to God by faith.[27] It means believing what God communicates to you and acting on it. Abraham believed what God told him and obeyed, and God counted this as righteousness: see Genesis 15:6; Romans 4:9; Galatians 3:6; James 2:21–22.

What is justice?

Easton's Bible Dictionary briefly defines *justice* as "rendering to every one that which is his due" (Easton).

---

26 Some interesting studies about the topic are shared at
   http://refbible.com/h/hospitality.htm.

27 See Romans 3:22; 4:5,9,11,13,22; 9:30; 10:6.

The *International Standard Bible Encyclopedia* explains it like this: "Justice has primarily to do with conduct in relation to others, especially with regard to the *rights* of others. In a larger sense *justice is not only giving to others their rights, but involves the active duty of establishing their rights.*" That last sentence is worth closer consideration:

If you want to be righteous, make it your duty to establish rights for those who don't have them.

Righteousness and justice are closely related[28] and are summed up in what Jesus calls the two greatest commandments: "'Love the Lord your God with all your heart and with all your soul and with all your mind.' This is the first and greatest commandment. And the second is like it: '*Love your neighbor as yourself*'" (Mt. 22:37–39 NIV).

Now let's *contrast* these godly values with the behavior of those who lived in the cities of the Plain.

Bad news begets bargaining

A bad report had reached heaven alarming enough that God needed to investigate the situation personally.

> [20]Then the Lord said, "How great is the *outcry* against Sodom and Gomorrah and how very grave their sin! [21]I must go down and see whether they have done altogether according to the outcry that has come to me; and if not, I will know."
> —*GENESIS 18:20–21*

---

28 See 1 Kings 10:9; 2 Chronicles 9:8; Job 29:14; 37:23; Psalm 33:5; 72:2; 97:2; 106:3; Proverbs 2:9; 8:20; 21:3; Isaiah 1:27; 5:16; 9:7; 28:17; 32:1,16; 33:5; Jeremiah 9:24; 22:3,15; 23:5; 33:15; Hosea 2:19; Amos 5:24; Wisdom 5:18; 8:7.

The Lord explains to Abraham that the outcry against these cities is great and their sin grievous. *Outcry* means an uproar, a shriek, a crying out in despair, a vehement public protest, "a cry for help in the face of distress" (Harris, Archer and Waltke, 570).

If God heard an outcry, there must have been many crying out to him in despair and protest about how they were treated. This implies that *the citizens of Sodom and Gomorrah were doing some rotten things to others*, and God became aware of the complaints.

If you are treated unfairly while traveling, you may grumble to yourself, complain to those who offended you or, if the crime is serious enough, report it to the governing authorities. Beyond these avenues, or having found no recourse, if you have been wronged greatly enough you may cry out to God for justice.

The outcry was not that of an individual, but of many people over time. Apparently, governing authorities in the Plain cities were refusing the wronged an audience; perhaps they were part of the oppression.

Considering that Israel—God's own people—cried out to him in the misery of Egyptian bondage for over 400 years (Ex. 2:23-25), the outcry against Sodom and Gomorrah was serious and significant. Great crimes had been committed, and God sent representatives to make a determination about the clamor. Their sin was "very grave": hard, grievous, heavy (Harris, Archer and Waltke, 943).

Two of the visitors depart toward Sodom to experience firsthand if the reports are true, but the one called "the Lord" remains with Abraham, who poses a question.

²³Then Abraham came near and said, "Will you indeed sweep away the righteous with the wicked? ²⁴Suppose there are fifty righteous within the city; will you then sweep away the place and not forgive it for the fifty righteous who are in it?"
—GENESIS 18:23-24

For all his deference at the visitors' arrival, Abraham becomes bold and draws near to the Lord—close enough to touch, kiss, or embrace (Harris, Archer and Waltke, 1297).

Although nothing has been said about divine judgment or destruction, Abraham importunately asks the Lord: *Will you destroy the righteous with the wicked?*

To destroy or sweep away is *sapâ*, meaning, "to scrape, shave, remove, or ruin" (Strong's H5595), and is "usually used in a hostile sense, particularly in contexts of judgment" (Harris, Archer and Waltke, 1531).

Without waiting, Abraham provides his own answer:

²⁵"Far be it from you to do such a thing, to slay the righteous with the wicked, so that the righteous fare as the wicked! Far be that from you! Shall not the Judge of all the earth do what is just?" ²⁶And the Lord said, "If I find at Sodom fifty righteous in the city, I will forgive the whole place for their sake."
—GENESIS 18:25-26

The Lord confirms that he will not destroy the city if He can find fifty righteous people there, reassuring Abraham that He is both merciful and just (Gen. 18:23). Abraham continues to bargain with the Lord in verses 27–32, and the Lord finally promises him, "For the sake of ten I will not destroy it" (v. 31).

After the Lord finishes speaking with his friend face to face[29], the Lord goes on his way, and Abraham "returns to his place." He steps back from the place of intercession, for he has surely extended himself into the Lord's grace on behalf of Lot and the people of Sodom, whom he had liberated in the Valley of Shaveh.

Why did Abraham intercede for Sodom?

Abraham bargains with the Lord to spare the city if only ten righteous people can be found there. Why? Because he hopes to save Lot and his family.

Will Lot and his family be spared? What happens to the two divine investigators once they reach the city?

Let's find out in the next chapter.

---

29 See Exodus 33:11.

6. Angels Arrive in Sodom

Genesis picks up the story when the two angels arrive in the city as the sun is setting.

> The two angels came to Sodom in the evening, and Lot was sitting in the gateway of Sodom. When Lot saw them, he rose to meet them, and bowed down with his face to the ground.
> —*GENESIS 19:1*

Disguised as ordinary travelers, the two angelic visitors arrive at the gateway of Sodom. Because they are travelers, they need lodging.

They meet Abraham's nephew Lot at the city gateway, "the seat of justice, of social intercourse and amusement, especially a favorite lounge in the evenings, the arched roof affording a pleasant shade" (Jamieson, Fausset and Brown, Gen. 19:1).

> When the two angels came to Sodom to warn Lot of the impending doom, they found him sitting in the city gate (Gn 19:1). This indicates that Sodom was fortified. Bab edh-Dhra, which means "gate of the arm," had imposing fortifications. The city wall, enclosing an area of 9–10 acres, was a massive 7 m (23 ft) wide and made of stones and mud bricks (Schaub 1993: 134). Evidence for settlement was found outside the walls as well. (Wood)

Where was the gate located? Archaeologists tell us that the gate in use at Sodom/Bab edh-Dhra during that time was located on the northeast side of the city.[30] (The western gate and wall had been destroyed previously and blocked up.)

A city gateway served as the administrative and judicial center where legal matters were discussed and prosecuted. This indicates that Lot may have been courting Sodom's ruling council. Regardless of his position, how did Lot act when he encountered these sojourning strangers?

Lot shows the strangers righteous hospitality

[1]The two angels came to Sodom in the evening, and Lot was sitting in the gateway of Sodom. When Lot saw them, *he rose to meet them, and bowed down with his face to the ground.* [2]He said, "Please, my lords, turn aside to your servant's house and spend the night, and wash your feet; then you can rise early and go on your way." They said, "No; we will spend the night in the square." [3]But he urged them strongly; so they turned aside to him and entered his house; and he made them a feast, and baked unleavened bread, and they ate.

—*GENESIS 19:1–3*

When Lot sees the visitors, he rises and *bows* to them as Abraham did (18:2). The word means to prostrate oneself (Strong's H7812). Lot shows these visitors the respect and hospitality his uncle offered them earlier. He addresses them deferentially as "my lords" and calls himself their "servant" as

---

30 "The [northeastern] gateway was comprised of two flanking towers with massive stone and timber foundations. They were ca. 4 m (13 ft) wide and 10 m (33 ft) long, with a 3–4 m (10–13 ft) passageway between" (Wood).

Abraham did. He asks them to sojourn at his home, where he would refresh them and give them lodging for the night.

They decline, saying they want to spend the night in the public square. "In many warm climates it was customary to sleep in the open air" (Dake, Gen. 19:2). "Where there are no inns and no acquaintance, it is not uncommon for travellers to sleep in the street wrapped up in their cloaks" (Jamieson, Fausset and Brown, Gen. 19:2).

Lot, however, *insists they come home with him*, perhaps because the open square is an unsafe place after dark or he knows they will find no hospitality elsewhere.

"Urged them strongly" is the Hebrew word *pasar*, meaning "to peck at, press, push" stubbornly (Strong H6484). Rotherham's *Emphasized Bible* translates it: "he became exceeding urgent with them" (Rotherham). So they accompanied him home.[31]

As his uncle did earlier, Lot prepares a banquet for them. We see more *divine hospitality*—righteousness in action—Near Eastern style. Again, they eat.

Meanwhile, outside the walls of Lot's house, trouble is brewing. What happens to the divine visitors?

Sodom's "Welcome Committee" arrives

[4]But before [Lot and his visitors] lay down, the men of the city, the men of Sodom, *both young and old, all the people* to the last man, surrounded the house; [5]and they called to Lot,

---

31 "Houses at Bab edh-Dhra were of the typical Early Bronze Age 'broad room' style. They were rectangular, being about 5 m (16 ft) long and 2–3 m (7–10 ft) wide with an entrance in one of the long sides (Rast 1987b: 46)" (Wood).

"Where are the men who came to you tonight? Bring them
out to us, so that we may *know* them."

—GENESIS 19:4–5

Before Lot, his family, and his honored guests lie down for
sleep, "the men[32] of the city" came. *Men* is *enôsh*, which means
"a mortal," *not* a male individual (Strong's H582), "'man' in the
sense of 'mankind'" (Harris, Archer and Waltke, 136a).[33] Both old
(*zaqan*), referring to men and women (Strong's H2205), and *young*
(*naar*), referring to boys, girls, and servants (Strong's H5288) show
up.

"All the people" means "people (as a congregated unit),
collective troops or attendants" (Strong's H5971); "from the
common Semitic root *amam* meaning 'to comprehend or
include'; people in general" (Harris, Archer and Waltke, 1640a).[34] The
Holman Christian Standard Bible translates the phrase as "the
whole population." The KJV adds, "all the people from every
quarter." *Quarter* (*qâtseh*) means "extremity, border, edge,
outmost coast" (Strong's H7097).

**The citizens who showed up at Lot's house were
not only men. EVERYONE was included—the
young and old, both males and females. They
came from every part of the city, even from**

---

32 Although the word *men* is used, in ancient cultures women, when
     present, were often not counted. For example, Matthew 14:21 mentions
     that, when Jesus fed the multitude with loaves and fishes, "The number
     of those who ate was about five thousand men, *besides women and
     children*" (NIV).

33 It is the same word used in Genesis 13:13.

34 See Genesis 14:21.

**its outermost borders and extremities.
Whatever they came for, it was
something that every citizen
of the city participated in.**

All the people surrounded the house. They called out to Lot, asking, "Where are the individuals who came to you tonight?" The word used is *enôsh*, meaning "people, in general."

Women and young people, as well men, gathered from the furthermost parts of the city at Lot's door. Why?

So that we may know them

The New International Version and other translations use the phrase "so that we can have sex with them." This is *not* found in other translations, nor is it in the Hebrew. The correct translation is "to know," as is translated in the New Revised Standard Version.[35]

The Hebrew word *yada*, "to know" (Strong's H3045) is used of knowledge in the vast majority of instances where some form of the word appears in the Old Testament. It "expresses a multitude of shades of knowledge gained by the senses" (Harris, Archer and Waltke, 848). It is rarely used to refer to the act of intercourse, and in many of these instances where it is used, it pertains to intimacy of which sexual relations are only a part.

The word *yada* occurs 944 times in the Old Testament. Only ten times—1% of the occurrences—could it be said to refer to intercourse, and *only heterosexual intercourse*. "In all

---

35 Also the BRG, Darby, DRA, ESV, GNV, JUB, KJV, LEB, RSV, YLT.

but ten times, it means *to be acquainted with*, to observe, to recognize, to have an understanding" (Kader 16). For example, "The ox *knows* its owner, and the donkey its master's crib; but Israel does not *know*, my people do not understand" (Isa. 1:3).

In many Bible versions, *yada* is translated in Genesis 19:5 as "sex" because of the predetermined bias of biblical translation committees. This can be determined by the way *yada* is translated in its *other* uses, which more clearly refer to intimacy leading to sexual relations. One such instance is Genesis 4:1: "Now Adam *knew* [*yada*] Eve his wife, and she conceived and bore Cain" (NKJV). The majority of other English translations use "knew" instead of sex in this Genesis 4:1.[36]

Why is the same word *yada* translated as "sex" in Genesis 19:5 where such a meaning is questionable, but translated as "knew" in its remaining its uses where sexual relations are obvious?

The Living Bible paraphrases it as, "Bring out those men to us so we can *rape* them." This perhaps is not far from the intent of the citizens of Sodom, but it is a poor translation for *yada*. Why wasn't *shakab* used? *Shakab* means "to lie down for rest or sexual connection" (Strong's H7901). Whenever *shakab* is used in a sexual sense, it refers to illicit relations (Harris, Archer and Waltke, 2381).[37] But *shakab* was not used in connection to the citizens of Sodom; *yada* was used.

Considering that both male and female, young and old are among those making the request, translating *yada* in a sexual

---

36 See also Numbers 31:17,35; Judges 11:39; 1 Kings 1:4; 1 Samuel 1:19.

37 See Genesis 19:32ff; 34:2,7; 35:22; Exodus 22:16; Deuteronomy 22:22; 27:21; Leviticus 18:22; 20:13; 1 Samuel 2:22; 2 Samuel 11:4.

sense—and primarily as homosexual sex—is puzzling. "[T]he sexual overtones to the story are minor, if present" (Boswell 93).

Interpreting the citizens' request as a demand for homosexual relations was not found in any pre-Christian Judaistic writings for the previous 2000 years; the first recorded instance of homosexual sex being connected to the Hebrew word *yada* is in Philo's *Quaest. Et Salut. in Genesis IV.31–37* (McNeill 72), and Philo wrote during Jesus' lifetime. We'll examine this issue further in "Historical Views About the Sin of Sodom and Gomorrah" on page 119.

Since about the twelfth century, this biblical story has been used to condemn homosexuality. The word *sodomy* was coined after the name of this city and the behavior of its inhabitants. Traditionalists claim and defend that God destroyed Sodom and Gomorrah because of homosexual activity. But we must continue to examine this passage carefully as well as look at *all* the verses about Sodom in the Bible, which we'll do in coming chapters.

How does Lot respond to the mob at his door?

Lot's response to the demands of wicked citizens

⁶Lot went out of the door to the men, shut the door after him, ⁷and said, "I beg you, my brothers, do not act so wickedly."
—GENESIS 19:6–7

Lot goes out to them, shutting the door behind himself and denying the citizens access to his visitors. Because of the Eastern code of hospitality, Lot was duty-bound to protect his guests. This code of hospitality among ancient Arab and Semitic peoples was so strict—considered sacred—that no one was permitted to harm even an enemy who had been offered shelter for the night (NIVSB). (See Deuteronomy 23:3–4 for an indication of how God feels about those who refuse to offer hospitality.)

Lot appeals to them as *brothers, ah*, meaning "brother, relative, fellow countrymen, friend, neighbor" (Harris, Archer and Waltke, 62a).

He begs them not to "act so wickedly." The Hebrew *ra'a* means "to spoil; to be good for nothing; to be bad physically, socially, or morally; to afflict; to do harm" (Strong's H7489). The essential meaning of this word can be understood by its frequent juxtaposition with the word *tob*, meaning "good." Moses said, "'See, I have set before you today life and good [*tob*], death and evil [*ra'a*]'" (Dt. 30:15 NKJV).

Lot apparently recognizes what the people are really there for. How would he know this, if not by previous experience?

What do the citizens really want?

Apparently, word had spread that two foreign visitors— *strangers*—had come to their city. We can't be sure whether the people of Sodom merely wanted to know more about the guests, but we learn they were unhappy about the visit and about Lot's behavior toward the sojourners.

From previous experience, Lot seems to know what the citizens of Sodom want with the strangers in their midst, and he realizes he must appease them. He says,

> "Look, I have two daughters who have not known a man; let me bring them out to you, and do to them as you please; only

do nothing to these men, for they have come under the shelter of my roof."
—GENESIS 19:8

Instead of his visitors, Lot offers to send out his two daughters "who have not *known* [yada] a *man* [îsh]." In this context the meaning of *yada* indicates the knowledge of intimacy that leads to sexual relations; Lot's daughters were unmarried virgins, although they were betrothed (Gen. 19:14).

The word for *man* here is *îsh*, meaning "a man as an individual or a male" (Strong's H376).[38] Lot says the people of Sodom could do with his daughters what "is good [tob] in your eyes." Of these people it could be said, "Woe to those who call evil [ra'a] good [tob] and good evil, who substitute darkness for light and light for darkness…" (Isa. 5:20 HCSB).

Lot begs, "Only do nothing to these *men*," enôsh (people), referring to the angelic visitors, "*for* they have come under the shelter of my roof." *For* means *because.* It is translated in the REB as "on this account." *Because* these visitors have taken shelter under his roof, they are protected by the divine code of hospitality by which Lot and Abraham lived.

The Lord was already inclined to punish Sodom before the angels arrived (see Genesis 13:13; 18:20–23). He considered inhospitality toward strangers a serious sin.[39]

---

38 Note that this word *îsh* was not used previously to describe the "men" of Sodom, because the writer was referring to people in general, *enôsh*.

39 See Deuteronomy 23:3–4; Job 29:16; 31:32; Matthew 25:35; Hebrews 13:2.

It should be remembered, moreover, that in the ancient world inns were rare outside of urban centers, and travelers were dependent on the hospitality and goodwill of strangers not just for comfort but for physical survival. Ethical codes almost invariably enjoined hospitality on their adherents as a sacred obligation (Boswell 96).

Church father Origen points out Lot's only righteous act:

Hear this, you who close your homes to guests! Hear this, you who shun the traveler as an enemy! Lot lived among the Sodomites. We do not read of any other good deeds of his: ...*he escaped the flames, escaped the fire, on account of one thing only. He opened his home to guests.* The angels entered the hospitable household; the flames entered those homes closed to guests. (Homilia V in Genesim [PG, 12:188–189]).

The value of women in ancient Near Eastern cultures

Present-day followers of the Lord may wonder about the propriety of a man exposing his virgin daughters to potential violence and abuse. This is another area, however, where the values of ancient cultures differ drastically from those we hold today.

Near Eastern societies of 4000 years ago valued men and their honor much more highly than that of women. Even St. Augustine, born in the fourth century A.D., wrote, "The body of a man is as superior to that of a woman as the soul is to the body" (De Mend. 7.10). As shocking as this sounds, we must realize that the equality of females is only a very recent development in the history of humankind.

During ancient times, women were considered to be *prop-erty*—see Exodus 22:16–17; Deuteronomy 22:28–29.

> In the mind of the Hebrew Testament, adultery is not an offense against a woman nor against the intimacy of marriage nor against the inherent requirements of sex. Adultery is an offense against justice. Adultery offends the man to whom the woman belongs. *Adultery is the misuse of another man's property* (Helminiak 49, emphasis mine).

The perceived worth and honor of men trumped that of women in the ancient world, and the honor of guests trumped both. The laws of hospitality demanded that Lot protect the male honor of his guests; in that world it was better that women be raped than men (Carden 35). Lot protected his visitors, offering his own daughters to appease the mob.

Yet, are the citizens of Sodom simply demanding some new flesh for their sexual pleasure? The only consideration that points to any sexual desire on the part of Sodom's citizens is Lot's offering them his daughters, which they refuse. But it is the most valuable bribe he could make to appease the hostile crowd.

Such an action is unthinkable in modern Western society, but females, and especially female children, held low status in the ancient world. "[E]ven in the more 'civilized' Roman world: Ammianus Marcellinus recounts... where the Roman consul Tertullus offers his children to an angry crowd to save himself. There is no sexual interest of any sort in the incident" (Boswell 95).

Sodom's hatred of strangers

Even if the citizens did want to have sex with them, what *kind* of sex is in question? The attitude of the mob gives us a clue.

> But they replied [to Lot], "Stand back!" And they said, "This fellow [Lot] came here as an *alien*, and he would play the judge! Now we will deal worse with you than with them." Then they pressed hard against the man Lot, and came near the door to break it down.
> —*Genesis 19:9*

They cry, "Stand back, get out of our way!" These people are pushy, demanding. They point out that Lot himself is an outsider, an alien, a foreigner.

Alien is the Hebrew *gûr*, meaning "to turn aside from the road (for a lodging or for any other purpose), i.e., sojourn (as a guest); also to shrink, fear (as in a strange place); also to gather for hostility (as afraid)" (Strong's H1481).

> The root means to live among people who are not blood relatives; thus, rather than enjoying native civil rights, *the ger was dependent on the hospitality that played an important role in the ancient near east; someone who did not enjoy the rights usually possessed by the resident*" (Harris, Archer and Waltke, 330, emphasis mine).

Judge is *shapat*, meaning, "to pronounce sentence; by extension to govern" (Strong's H8199), and "to exercise the processes of government; to act as ruler; to decide cases of controversy as judge" (Harris, Archer and Waltke, 2443).

It seems the citizens of Sodom resent Lot because he is making decisions—showing hospitality to and protecting sojourning strangers—against the customs of the city, taking authority where he has none.

Lot's insistence on the protection of his visitors according to the divine law of hospitality angers the residents of Sodom. They point out that he came to their city as a sojourner, someone who has no rights in their estimation, but who is now putting on airs to act as a judge and ruler by setting policy concerning how visitors are treated.

Note their mistrust, hostility, and disrespect of foreigners and their prejudice against *outsiders*—the antithesis of Abraham's and Lot's behavior toward strangers. It seems they plan to treat these visitors as they have treated all other visitors, perhaps those whose outcry God had heard.

Lot has whisked two visiting strangers from the city gate to his home. He refuses to turn them over to the mob. The people of Sodom perhaps perceive the visitors as hostile, consider them to be spies. Maybe they think Lot is trying to subvert their city. (They seem to have been at odds with Lot about the subject before this.) They simply may want to learn who the visitors are and examine their credentials. They are highly disturbed upon hearing the rumors that obviously spread like wildfire through the city. Because of this, they become violent and threaten to "deal worse" (*ra'a*, evil) with Lot than with his visitors.

The mob "pressed hard"—with exceeding vehemence—against Lot, attacking him to break down the door.

What do the citizens want? If they are simply lusting for recreational sex, why are they so *menacing*? Why do they threaten to harm Lot? If he has lived there for some time, why haven't they harmed him before this? These people are angry, abusive, and violent. But why?

The crucial questions to ask about this passage are:

- *Why* do the inhabitants of Sodom threaten to harm Lot and abuse his guests?
- What is their *motivation*?

We can discover the answers by looking closer to home, at least in time.

If only we could say the answer to Sodom's behavior is a thing of the ancient past. Unfortunately, it is still happening today.

7. Torture and Abuse at Abu Ghraib Prison

Why did American soldiers—both men and women—abuse, torture, molest, and rape Iraqi prisoners at Abu Ghraib prison in Baghdad in 2003? As you ponder this question, follow these links with discretion:

https://en.wikipedia.org/wiki/Abu_Ghraib_torture_and_prisoner_abuse

https://en.wikipedia.org/wiki/Abu_Ghraib_prison

http://www.cnn.com/2013/10/30/world/meast/iraq-prison-abuse-scandal-fast-facts/

Perhaps the people of Sodom had the same attitude and objectives as the U.S. soldiers at Baghdad Central Prison:

- **Primary:** Interrogation—knowledge
- **Secondary:** Sexual abuse—degradation

The kind of sex the inhabitants of Sodom wanted was not for sensual pleasure, but for domination, control, cruelty, humiliation, debasement and abuse.

This kind of treatment isn't about sex; it's about racial and imperialistic arrogance that revels in the degradation of foreigners, outsiders, and strangers. It's xenophobia.

Sex as a weapon

In ancient cultures, forcing sex on other men was a way of besting them, of humiliating them and showing them who's boss.

For instance, during war, besides raping the women and sometimes slaughtering children, victors cut off the garments of the defeated men, exposing their buttocks, and then chained them and paraded them through the streets to debase and humiliate them.[40] In Ancient Athens, "male rape was employed to signify the victory over foreign enemies in war" (Carden 35).

> Rather than representing sexual desire and erotic expression, *rape is best understood as sexual violence intended to assert power or express anger*.... As an assertion of power, rape is a weapon in the power dynamics of male sexuality and patriarchal gender relations. ... [M]ale rapists are primarily *heterosexual* men (McMullen 1990: 118). ... In Western society, then, male rape reinforces the heterosexuality of the rapist while casting that of the victim in doubt (Carden 33, emphasis mine).

Sometimes conquerors would rape the men—not because the perpetrators were gay or took passionate pleasure in homosexual acts—but because *it was the ultimate humiliation*

---

40 See http://jrscience.wcp.muohio.edu/Research/ HNatureProposalsArticles/RapeWarfare.html; http:// library.flawlesslogic.com/massrape.htm; https://en.wikipedia.org/wiki/ Homosexuality_in_ancient_Rome; http://www.williamapercy.com/ wiki/images/Rape.pdf; http://ejil.oxfordjournals.org/content/18/2/ 253.full.

to treat the enemy as women, who in that day were considered little more than property. In essence, it was a way of treating the abused men like *slaves*.

Among some macho heterosexual men today (as well as school children), the ultimate putdown is to call another guy a "fag." In ancient times, it was to call a man a "woman" and to treat him like one sexually.

Rape, a tactic of degradation

Did the abusive soldiers at Abu Ghraib do what they did because they all had a homosexual orientation? Did they strip and molest prisoners of *both* sexes because they were otherwise incapable of healthy sexual relations with a person they cared about?

In both Sodom and Baghdad, the horrible acts that took place were not expressions of homosexual orientation.

> In ancient Babylonian sex-divination texts, anal sex is regarded as a power relationship by which the penetrator is either advanced or diminished according to the status of the men he penetrates. ... Throughout [Greenberg's] survey it becomes clear that, in the ancient Mediterranean world, the act of penetrating other males did not stigmatize the penetrator and that male-male anal sex was considered *an act of aggression by which the penetrated male is feminized by the penetrator*. ... [H]e also notes that *male rape was employed as a form of punishment* (Carden 31, emphasis mine).

The people of Sodom weren't looking for recreational sex. They wanted to perpetrate a violent act of humiliation and abuse visiting strangers who, as a class, they had no respect for. Rape was only the *means* to degradation.

Ostensibly, this was their common practice, and the cities of the Plain had structured their entire society around it. But their degrading behavior was the opposite of the righteous hospitality that Abraham and Lot showed these outsiders.

> [T]he incident clearly indicates that strangers may not be welcome, or have no rights, in Sodom. Attempted rape here is illustrative of the evils of inhospitality and abuse of outsiders that are typical of Sodom (Carden 21).

Like the misguided soldiers at Abu Ghraib prison, the crime of the people of Sodom wasn't their sexual orientation, but their *xenophobic prejudice and shameless contempt for human rights and debasement of outsiders, individuals unlike themselves.*

God commanded Israel, "Do not mistreat an alien or oppress him, for you were aliens in Egypt" (Ex. 22:21 NIV). The people of Sodom flagrantly violated a value dear to the heart of God.

The Sodom and Gomorrah account is not the only one that deals with such ungodly mistreatment. To get to the ultimate meaning of the Genesis 19 account, we must study a similar passage in Judges 19.

8. A Stranger Comes to Gibeah

An account of abuse strangely similar to that of Sodom is recorded in Judges 19, although the only person who ends up being harmed is a woman.

Chapters 19 through 21 of Judges recount one of the most heinous crimes recorded in all of Scripture. We'll examine portions of this passage to see how it relates to the Sodom account.

> ¹In those days, when there was no king in Israel, a certain Levite, residing in the remote parts of the hill country of Ephraim, took to himself a concubine from Bethlehem in Judah. ²But his concubine became angry with him, and she went away from him to her father's house at Bethlehem in Judah, and was there some four months. ³Then her husband set out after her, to speak tenderly to her and bring her back. He had with him his servant and a couple of donkeys. When he reached her father's house, the girl's father saw him and came with joy to meet him. ⁴His father-in-law, the girl's father, made him stay, and he remained with him three days; so they ate and drank, and he stayed there.
> —*JUDGES 19:1–4*

A Levite from the tribal territory of Ephraim had taken a concubine—a second wife. Concubines were like first wives, only their offspring received no inheritance from the father. In those days, having concubines was customary. Both wives and concubines were considered property of the man. The *Expanded Bible* calls her "a slave woman."

This Levite's concubine had left him to return to her own family in Bethlehem. After four months of separation, the Levite travels to Bethlehem to persuade her to reconcile with him. He takes his servant and two donkeys with him. (Taking two donkeys indicates he is determined to bring her back with him.)

Father delays their departure

The concubine's father welcomes the Levite and, showing generous hospitality, convinces him to stay in their home for three days. The Levite would return to Ephraim, but his father-in-law persuades them to stay two extra days. He would have them remain a sixth day, but on the evening of the fifth, the Levite refuses to stay the night.

> ⁹When the man with his concubine and his servant got up to leave, his father-in-law, the girl's father, said to him, "Look, the day has worn on until it is almost evening. Spend the night. See, the day has drawn to a close. Spend the night here and enjoy yourself. Tomorrow you can get up early in the morning for your journey, and go home."
> ¹⁰But the man would not spend the night; he got up and departed, and arrived opposite Jebus (that is, Jerusalem). He had with him a couple of saddled donkeys, and his concubine was with him.
> —*JUDGES 19:9–10*

The Levite refuses Jebus

Jebus was a city in Canaan that later became Jerusalem when King David and Joab took the city. At the time of this passage, however, neither the tribe of Judah nor Benjamin had been able to drive the Jebusites out of the high city.[41] In the era of Judges, this city and its surrounding area were already settled.

Jebus was a place where desert sojourners could lodge overnight (Miller and Lane 303). But the Levite does not want to stay there.

> [11]When they were near Jebus, the day was far spent, and the servant said to his master, "Come now, let us turn aside to this city of the Jebusites, and spend the night in it." [12]But his master said to him, "We will not turn aside into a city of *foreigners*, who do not belong to the people of Israel; but we will continue on to Gibeah." [13]Then he said to his servant, "Come, let us try to reach one of these places, and spend the night at Gibeah or at Ramah." [14]So they passed on and went their way; and the sun went down on them near Gibeah, which belongs to Benjamin. [15]They turned aside there, to go in and spend the night at Gibeah. He went in and sat down in the open square of the city, but no one took them in to spend the night.
>
> —*JUDGES 19:11–15 NIV*

The Levite doesn't want to stay in Jebus because it is controlled by foreigners. Instead, he desires to sojourn in a city belonging to his countrymen. Little does he know what lies in store for him from a tribe of his own people.

---

41 The Jebusites were a Canaanite people descended from the Amorites and Hittites (see Ezek. 16:3). They were the people who tricked Israel into making a covenant with them by wearing old clothes and showing them moldy bread in Joshua 9:1–15. They were a shrewd and persistent people that neither Judah (Josh. 15:63) nor Benjamin (Jdg. 1:21) could drive out of the city (Miller and Lane 303).

They arrive at Gibeah

They finally enter Gibeah, a city inhabited by Benjamites (another Israelite tribe). Gibeah may have had no public inn, for they camp out in the town square. No one provides them hospitality until an old man comes along.

An old man offers hospitality

¹⁶Then at evening there was an old man coming from his work in the field. The man was from the hill country of Ephraim, and he was residing in Gibeah. *(The people of the place were Benjaminites.)* ¹⁷When the old man looked up and saw the wayfarer in the open square of the city, he said, "Where are you going and where do you come from?" ¹⁸He answered him, "We are passing from Bethlehem in Judah to the remote parts of the hill country of Ephraim, from which I come. I went to Bethlehem in Judah; and I am going to my home. Nobody has offered to take me in. ¹⁹We your servants have straw and fodder for our donkeys, with bread and wine for me and the woman and the young man along with us. We need nothing more." ²⁰The old man said, "Peace be to you. I will care for all your wants; *only do not spend the night in the square.*" ²¹So he brought him into his house, and fed the donkeys; they washed their feet, and ate and drank.
—*JUDGES 19:16–21*

It is odd that the Levite chooses to stay in a town of his own people instead of in a city of strangers, yet finds no hospitality in that town except from a man from Ephraim who happens to be living there temporarily. The word *residing* in verse 16 is the Hebrew *gûr*, meaning "sojourner," as discussed previously.

The Hebrew word used for the old *man* is *îsh*, "a man as an individual or a male person" (Strong's H376).

Is this simply a nice man? Showing hospitality is an act of righteousness. But being a sojourner himself, this fellow may have been subject to prejudice and oppression by the native inhabitants of Gibeah and wanted to spare his visitors mistreatment or violence, as Lot did for the angels.

The Levite accepts hospitality

It seems the old man is warning the Levite and his party not to spend the night in the square. After exchanging social pleasantries, the Levite accepts the hospitality of the old man and goes home with him. There, the host tends to all the needs of his visitors, even though they already have all they require.

As mentioned previously, it was the custom of Eastern peoples to provide for their guests as if they were members of their own family or honored dignitaries. If you were an ancient Easterner, whoever came under your roof as a guest could expect your provision and protection, even unto death. This custom would soon be tried.

The children of Belial arrive

> [22]As they were making their hearts merry, behold, the men of the city, worthless fellows, surrounded the house, beating on the door. And they said to the old man, the master of the house, "Bring out the man who came into your house, that we may know him." [23]And the man, the master of the house, went out to them and said to them, "No, my brothers, do not act so wickedly; since this man has come into my house, do not do this vile thing."
>
> —JUDGES 19:22–23 ESV

The word *men* here is *enôsh*, meaning "a mortal, people in general" (Strong's H582), the same word used for the citizens of

Sodom who showed up at Lot's door. It includes both men and women.

The King James Version says that "certain *sons of Belial*, beset the house round about" (Jdg. 19:22). This phrase "sons of Belial" means "worthless fellows, scoundrels, sons of the devil, children of evil" (Miller and Lane 303).[42] *Sons* is *ben*, "not exclusively a reference to the male offspring of human parents," but an idiom "for children generally, for descendants" (Harris, Archer and Waltke, 254).

These wicked people, both men and women, are depraved. They discovered someone new in town and determine to dominate and debase him. This sounds much like the Genesis 19 account of the people of Sodom who demand audience with the angels who visited Lot.

The old man negotiates

Bound by the duty of hospitality, the old man slips outside and begs them not to abuse the Levite. He says, "No, my *brothers*...." Maybe he is simply trying to be persuasive. Perhaps he has dealt with this group before. In any event, he caters to their unholy spirit and compromises with them in order to protect his guest.

> "Look, here is my virgin daughter, and his concubine. I will bring them out to you now, and you can use them and do to

---

42 See also Deuteronomy 13:13; 1 Samuel 1:16; 2:12; 10:27; 25:17,25; 30:22; 2 Samuel 16:7; 20:1; 22:5; 23:6; 1 Kings 21:10–13; 2 Chronicles 13:17; Psalm 18:4; 101:3; Proverbs 6:12; 16:27; 19:28; Nahum 1:11,15.

them whatever you wish. But as for this man, don't do such an outrageous thing."

—*JUDGES 19:24 NIV*

The old man offers them his own virgin daughter, probably yet a teenager or younger, and the Levite's concubine. Note that he does *not* offer the young male servant.

Lot does the *same thing* the night the citizens of Sodom want to debase the angels. It may be that, because of previous dealings with these Benjamites, the old man knows if he doesn't appease them, he and his guest will be harmed.

The Gibeahites become violent

Verse 22 says the people surround the house and pound on the door. They mean business. The angels with Lot at Sodom rescue him and strike the wicked men with blindness, but there are no angels on the scene at the home of the old man in Gibeah.

For "use them," the KJV says, "humble them." The word *anâ* contains the meaning "the idea of looking down or browbeating, to debase, deal hardly with" (Strong's H6031). As in Sodom, the custom of Gibeah is to interrogate and humiliate foreigners and strangers in their midst as a show of superiority and domination.

But the men would not listen to him. So the man *took* his concubine and sent her outside to them, and they raped her and abused her throughout the night, and at dawn they let her go.

—*JUDGES 19:25 NIV*

Men here again is *enôsh*, "a mortal, people in general" (Strong's H582), the same word used in the Sodom account to refer to all the citizens, both men and women.

The Levite hands over his wife

To save his own skin, the Levite takes the concubine and throws her out to them. This word *took* is the Hebrew word *hazaq*, meaning, "to fasten upon, hence to seize; to bind, restrain, conquer" (Strong's H2388). The Levite *forces* his wife outside to appease these people. Because the concubine has to be forced outside, she must not have wanted to go.

This Levite, a man from the priestly tribe of Israel, traveled to Bethlehem determined to reclaim his slave wife. He convinces her to reconcile with him, and she leaves her father's household. Yet here in Gibeah he throws her to the wolves to be abused.

The word *abused* is *alal*: "by implication (in a bad sense) to overdo, i.e. maltreat" (Strong's H5953).

[To] deal with severely, abuse, make a fool of someone, mock. It is used to indicate the exercise of power over another person, generally in a bad sense, hence meaning 'to maltreat.' It signifies some great achievement, generally malevolent. *This word is used to depict the exploitation of one person by another* (Harris, Archer and Waltke, 1627, emphasis mine).

The woman was a slave, the man's property. Nonetheless her husband forces her out, and the people of Gibeah mistreat and abuse her all through the night to the point of overdoing it.

The concubine meets her fate

As morning appeared, the woman came and fell down at the door of the man's house where her master was, until it was light.

—*JUDGES 19:26*

Who knows where the people of Gibeah had taken her, how many of them had been with her, and what shocking crimes they had perpetrated upon her. But she made it back alive. Perhaps she pounded on the door just as the people who had abused her had pounded on it the evening before. If she did, no one answered.

> [27]When her master got up in the morning and opened the door of the house and stepped out to continue on his way, there lay his concubine, fallen in the doorway of the house, with her hands on the threshold. [28]He said to her, "Get up; let's go." But there was no answer. Then the man put her on his donkey and set out for home.
>
> —*JUDGES 19:27–28 NIV*

After a good's night rest, the Levite leaves the old man's house to continue on his way to Ephraim. But there lies his wife on the stoop with her hands on the threshold!

As if nothing has happened, he says to her, "Get up! Let's get moving!" She doesn't answer. He rolls her over and discovers she is dead. He throws her over his donkey and heads for home.

The Levite demands justice

[29]When he reached home, he *took* a knife and cut up his concubine, limb by limb, into twelve parts and sent them

into all the areas of Israel. ³⁰Everyone who saw it was saying to one another, "Such a thing has never been seen or done, not since the day the Israelites came up out of Egypt. Just imagine! We must do something! So speak up!"

—*JUDGES 19:29–30 NIV*

The word *took* here is again *hazaq*, meaning, "to seize" (Strong's H2388), the same word used in his throwing her out the old man's door. The Levite, who so callously forced his recently reunited wife out the door into the night, chops her corpse into twelve pieces, one for each of the tribes of Israel. He sends each piece with information about the atrocious crime that the men of Gibeah committed, calling for vengeance upon them (see Deuteronomy 23:17 KJV).

How ironic it is that the man whom God uses to bring Israel to attention about its moral depravity is himself so cold-hearted and uncaring. The people of Israel are outraged and roused to action.

Israel responds in outrage

¹Then all Israel from Dan to Beersheba and from the land of Gilead came together as one and assembled before the Lord in Mizpah. ²The leaders of all the people of the tribes of Israel took their places in the assembly of God's people, four hundred thousand men armed with swords. ³(The Benjamites heard that the Israelites had gone up to Mizpah.) Then the Israelites said, "Tell us how this awful thing happened."

⁴So the Levite, the husband of the murdered woman, said, "I and my concubine came to Gibeah in Benjamin to spend the night. ⁵During the night the men of Gibeah came after me

and surrounded the house, intending to kill me. They raped my concubine, and she died."

—*JUDGES 20:1–5 NIV*

The people of Israel gather to take action against this hideous crime. They want to hear the full story. The Levite reveals that the intent of the people of Gibeah was to kill him. If they had merely wanted homosexual relations, they would not have settled for the female concubine, preferring instead the male slave.

Moral of the story: xenophobia leads to abuse

Boswell points out that "Jews and Christians have overwhelmingly failed to interpret this story as one of homosexuality, correctly assessing it as a moral about inhospitality" (Boswell 95–96). Why is this account not treated the same as the Sodom story in the eyes of believers today?

This passage isn't considered an indictment of homosexuality because it focuses on the fate of the concubine, a *woman*.

> Her fate shows that the men of Gibeah were not animated by overwhelming homosexual desire. ... The men of Gibeah did not turn up to invite the Levite to an orgy, and the concubine had no power over what befell her. There can be no doubt that this story is one about attempted pack rape of a man, which is diverted into the successful pack rape of a woman.
>
> *Pack rape of a defenceless stranger is a particularly apt symbol of injustice and abuse of the helpless, which I would argue are the real sins of Sodom and Gibeah and not same-sex desire....* It is not the gender of the victims that is crucial, but their status, that of defenceless aliens. (Carden 25–26, emphasis mine).

The wicked Gibeahites accept only the *Levite's* concubine and not the host's virgin daughter. "To the mob, the Levite is clearly outsider, and the concubine is his woman and shares his outsider status. She is therefore a suitable substitute while the old man's daughter is not" (Carden 37).

Israel reacts to the crime

In Judges 20:8–11, the people of Israel gather in Gibeah to mete out vengeance. They demand that the Benjamites surrender the wicked people so they may be put to death. Then Israel will be purged of the offense.

The Benjamites refuse to listen to the other tribes of Israel. Instead, they decide to fight.

Benjamin, the ravenous wolf

In Genesis 49:27, the tribe of Benjamin is referred to as a "ravenous wolf" (NIV). Gibeah of Benjamin was a city of such people who had corrupted their way and turned courage and cunning into perversion, vice, and violence.

> ¹Woe to the city of oppressors, rebellious and defiled!
>
> ²*She obeys no one, she accepts no correction.* She does not trust in the Lord, she does not draw near to her God.
>
> ³*Her officials within her are roaring lions; her rulers are evening wolves, who leave nothing for the morning.*
>
> —ZEPHANIAH 3:1–3 NIV

Does this not characterize the wicked people of Gibeah? They prowled as wolves in the night, and left nothing of the poor concubine in the morning. God says such a city is defiled.

Israel battles the Benjamites

Benjamin musters its forces against those of Israel, who sends the tribe of Judah first, at the Lord's direction. Even though Israel has 400,000 soldiers and Benjamin only 26,700, the Benjamites slaughter 22,000 Israelites but lose none of their own men.

It must have been difficult for the men of Israel to fight against their own brother-tribe, especially after they had suffered such a defeat. They weep before the Lord and seek His counsel. God says, "Go up against them again."

On the second day of fighting, Israel loses 18,000 more valiant men to the Benjamites. How much harder it must have been to face for the second time this kind of defeat against wicked, rebellious people. This time, the Israelites weep before the Lord, fasting and offering burnt offerings and fellowship offerings to Him.

> [27]And the Israelites inquired of the Lord. (In those days the ark of the covenant of God was there, [28]with Phinehas son of Eleazar, the son of Aaron, ministering before it.) They asked, "Shall we go up again to fight against the Benjamites, our fellow Israelites, or not?"
> The Lord responded, "Go, for tomorrow I will give them into your hands."
> —JUDGES 20:27–28 NIV

Israel ambushes Gibeah and draws the Benjamites away from the city. Israel loses thirty more men, but God gives them a strategy to defeat the Benjamites.

Out of 26,700 men, 25,100 Benjamites fall to the sword on the third day, leaving only 1,600 warriors. The men of Israel chase them and all but annihilate them. Not only do the Benjamites lose their fighting men, but Israel destroys all their towns, their livestock, and everything they find. After the battle is over, the people of Israel grieve at the gruesome task of vengeance.

> ²The people went to Bethel, where they sat before God until evening, raising their voices and weeping bitterly. ³"Lord, God of Israel," they cried, "why has this happened to Israel? Why should one tribe be missing from Israel today?" …
> ⁶Now the Israelites grieved for the tribe of Benjamin, their fellow Israelites. "Today one tribe is cut off from Israel," they said.
>
> —*JUDGES 21:2–3,6 NIV*

Why did the Lord allow this to happen? Because perversion grows like leaven in human societies, spreading until all of its people are defiled.

God judges corrupt cities because their sin has the capacity to infect entire nations and bring them to downfall.

The men of Gibeah were not homosexuals. But they *were* inhospitable, violent, and abusive. They treated the visiting Levite—a foreigner and a stranger—the same way the people of Sodom dealt with Lot and his two guests.

Comparing Genesis 19 with Judges 19

In comparison, the Judges 19 narrative is quite similar to the Genesis 19 account, but includes two serious crimes, one of which is brutal murder.

Both accounts begin with a description of sojourners, two outsiders who dwell in the midst of immoral cultures, two sets of visitors, two hospitable households, two confrontations by the local people, two threats of violence, and two devastating conclusions.

In both accounts, the violent demands of the local people are a way to denigrate the honorable moral values of the sojourners in their midst, values they did not share.

Neither Lot nor the old man of Gibeah defends his visitors to safeguard them from same-sex relations. "Instead," says Matthew Vines, "they both expressed the concern that their visitors had come under the protection of their homes" (Vines 66–67). Both shielded their guests because of the sacred code of hospitality.

Those who are righteous make it their duty to establish rights for those who don't have them, especially strangers and aliens.

Both accounts include hospitable hosts who believe it is more important to protect their guests over their own flesh and blood (daughters). But why?

> Some have argued that Lot's action revealed his belief that opposite-sex behavior was preferable to same-sex behavior. [It is true] that the gender of Lot's guests played a role—not because of Lot's concerns about the bodily "sameness" involved in same-sex behavior, but because of the greater honor men held in ancient times. ...[M]en in the ancient world were considered to be of greater value than women, which made raping a man a more serious violation. ... The issue in both instances is *patriarchy*, not the anatomical complementarity of men and women (Vines 67, emphasis mine).

The sexual sin in Judges, although *heterosexual* in nature, isn't fornication. It's violent abuse and rape. They abuse and rape a woman until she eventually dies.

The accounts differ, however, in their result. Both hosts offer women, considered to be of lesser honor and value than men. The people of Sodom refuse; the people of Gibeah accept, resulting in the sexual abuse and death of the concubine.

Another important difference is how present-day Bible believers interpret the stories and continue to use them to make moral arguments today.

In both accounts the locals demand the handing-over of male visitors and threaten violence. Although actual violence to the visiting men happens in neither story, *only the Sodom account* is remembered and rehearsed as representing the evils of homosexuality. The Gibeah account, if mentioned at all, is never interpreted this way.

The word *Sodomites* refers to the inhabitants of the city Sodom. But their crimes, inaccurately interpreted as an indictment against homosexuality, have taken on such proportion that *Sodomites* is now used to refer to those who practice homosexual acts—*sodomy*.

Why hasn't the same process of abstraction happened for the word *Benjamites* or *Gibeahites*?

Christian theology did not become preoccupied with a "sin of the Benjamites" (as the inhabitants of Gibeah were called), nor did European countries adopt penal statues against "Benjamy." This is more striking because the incidents at Gibeah are more horrible than the events surrounding Lot's hospitality to the angelic messengers in Sodom. The citizens of Sodom do nothing in the end. They are blinded by the angels, who then instruct Lot to hurry his family out of the city in view of its impending destruction. At Gibeah, there are no angels to rescue the sacrificed woman during the dark night of her torture. Nor does God punish Gibeah with a fiery storm. The Israelite armies must do it themselves, after sustaining heavy casualties. Why is it then that the story of Sodom had such a long afterlife? How does it come to be misread so systematically and for so many centuries? The beginning of an answer lies precisely in the dramatic and total divine judgment executed on the city and its neighbors. (Jordan 30–31).

The sin of Sodom wasn't men having sex with other men.

Their sin was the abuse, degradation, and violation of others, STRANGERS—the same sin as men of Gibeah committed—although the Gibeahites raped a woman.

The Sodom story has taken on a life of its own because of the fiery judgment it ends with. This makes it imperative that it be interpreted correctly and not misread as it has been and continues to be to this day. Let's investigate further.

9. The Fate of Lot and His Family

We left Lot standing outside his door in Sodom, arguing with a violent mob that's trying to break down the door. What happens next?

> [10]But the men inside reached out their hands and brought Lot into the house with them, and shut the door. [11]And they struck with blindness the men who were at the door of the house, *both small and great*, so that they were unable to find the door.
> —GENESIS 19:10–11

The angels rescue Lot and strike the mob with sudden blindness. Again, the word for *men* here is enôsh, "a mortal, people in general" (Strong's H582), both *small*, qâtân, "little, young" (Strong's H6996), and *great*, gadôl, "older" (Strong's H1419)—all the citizens who had gathered from every part of the city (Gen. 19:4 KJV).

Lot's future sons-in-laws left behind

> [12]Then the men said to Lot, "Have you anyone else here? Sons-in-law, sons, daughters, or anyone you have in the city—bring them out of the place. [13]For we are about to destroy this place, because the outcry against its people has become great before the Lord, and the Lord has sent us to destroy it." [14]So Lot *went out* and said to his sons-in-law, who were to marry his daughters, "Up, get out of this place; for

the Lord is about to destroy the city." But he seemed to his sons-in-law to be jesting.
—GENESIS 19:12–14

There is no record of Lot having sons, but his virgin daughters were both betrothed. Lot "went out," meaning he left the house and went to the homes of his sons-in-law. Note that they were *not* part of the mob outside his door. Although he told them plainly what was about to happen, they unfortunately did not believe him and failed to heed his warning to flee the city.

> [15]When morning dawned, the angels urged Lot, saying, "Get up, take your wife and your two daughters who are here, or else you will be consumed in the punishment of the city." [16]But he lingered; so the men seized him and his wife and his two daughters by the hand, the Lord being merciful to him, and they brought him out and left him outside the city. [17]When they had brought them outside, they said, "Flee for your life; do not look back or stop anywhere in the Plain; flee to the hills, or else you will be consumed."
> —GENESIS 19:15–17

Some hours have passed since the beginning of the trouble, for dawn comes. The angels must urge Lot to take his wife and daughters. Yet they hesitate, so the angels seize them by the hand—*hazaq* (Strong's H2388)—and lead them outside the city walls. They advise Lot to flee to the mountains without looking back.

Lot and family flee south to Zoar instead

[18]And Lot said to them, "Oh, no, my lords; [19]your servant has found favor with you, and you have shown me great

kindness in saving my life; but I cannot flee to the hills, for fear the disaster will overtake me and I die. ²⁰Look, that city is near enough to flee to, and it is a little one. Let me escape there—is it not a little one?—and my life will be saved!" ²¹He said to him, "Very well, I grant you this favor too, and will not overthrow the city of which you have spoken. ²²Hurry, escape there, for I can do nothing until you arrive there." Therefore the city was called Zoar. ²³The sun had risen on the earth when Lot came to Zoar.

—GENESIS 19:18–23

Although ten righteous people in Sodom could not be found, the Lord nonetheless delivers Lot and his daughters before destroying the cities of the Plain.

Lot fears fleeing to the hills, so he is permitted to escape to Zoar instead. When they reach this little town south of Sodom and Gomorrah, destruction comes.

10. Destruction of the Cities

Once Lot and his family reached the safety of Zoar, destruction came. How were the cities destroyed?

> [24]Then the Lord rained on Sodom and Gomorrah *sulfur and fire* from the Lord out of heaven; [25]and he *overthrew* those cities, and all the Plain, and all the inhabitants of the cities, and what grew on the ground. [26]But Lot's wife, behind him, looked back, and she became a pillar of salt.
>
> —GENESIS 19:24–26

In nearly forty instances of the word *rain* in the Bible, it "is never to be taken for granted by mankind; it comes from the hand of God... in amounts proportionate to the spiritual condition of the inhabitants of that land" (Harris, Archer and Waltke, 1187). In this instance, the Lord rained down not water, but "sulfur and fire... out of heaven."

> Upon the wicked He will rain coals; *fire and brimstone* and a burning wind shall be the portion of their cup.
>
> —PSALM 11:6 NKJV

The word *sulfur* (*brimstone* in the KJV) is the Hebrew goprît (Strong's H1614), which occurs seven times in the Old Testament.[43] The word *fire* is esh (Strong's H784), that typically used for fire, appearing 379 times in the OT.

The word *goprit* is a foreign loan word, most likely derived from Akkadian *ki/ubritu*, which means sulfurous oil (black sulfur) (Gentry 1999). The word accompanying *goprit*, *wc es*, simply means "and fire." In other words, the material that fell on Sodom and Gomorrah and the Cities of the Plain (except Zoar) was a burning petroleum product. The term *hapak* means to overturn, or overthrow. (Wood).

What was the fire? The word *esh* is used in Job 1:16, where it may indicate lightning: "While he was still speaking, another came and said, 'The *fire of God fell from heaven* and burned up the sheep and the servants, and consumed them; I alone have escaped to tell you.'" Lightning alone seems unlikely in the Genesis 19 account.

The sulfur, or brimstone, was a *burning petroleum product.* Bitumen pits are mentioned in Genesis 14:10, a petroleum product similar to asphalt that "was commonly found in the shallow southern basin of the Dead Sea in antiquity" (Wood).

Another possible explanation is volcanic eruption. However, Frederick G. Clapp's geologic investigations of the region in 1929 and 1934 found "no evidence to indicate that lava or ash eruptions had taken place as recently as 4000 years ago." The last possible eruption in the vicinity had taken place thousands of years before the time of Abraham (Wood).

But Clapp discovered that the region south of the Dead Sea was unstable, bordered by fault lines on the east and west. Earthquakes were common in this area. Clapp surveyed the geology of the district and, after finding bitumen and

---

43 See Deuteronomy 29:23; Job 18:15; Psalm 11:6; Isaiah 30:33; 34:9; Ezekiel 38:22.

petroleum in the area, concluded that "combustible materials from the earth destroyed the cities."

> Natural gas and sulfur, which normally accompany bitumen and petroleum, are also present. *These combustible materials could have been forced from the earth by subterranean pressure brought about by an earthquake resulting from the shifting of the bounding faults* (Clapp 1936a: 906; 1936b: 40). Geologists who have studied the area in recent times agree with Clapp's reconstruction (Harris and Beardow 1995: 360; Neev and Emery 1995: 13–14; 33, 37). *If lightning or surface fires ignited these combustibles as they came spewing forth from the ground, it would indeed result in a holocaust such as described in Genesis 19.* It is significant to note that both Bab edh-Dhra [Sodom] and Numeira [Gomorrah] lie at the edge of the plain, *exactly on the eastern fault line!* (Wood, emphasis mine)

Abraham, who interceded before the Lord for the deliverance of the cities of the Plain, looked down from Hebron across the Plain and witnessed the destruction.

> [27]Abraham went early in the morning to the place where he had stood before the Lord; [28]and he looked down toward Sodom and Gomorrah and toward all the land of the Plain and saw the smoke of the land going up like the smoke of a furnace.
>
> [29]So it was that, when God destroyed the cities of the Plain, God remembered Abraham, and sent Lot out of the midst of the overthrow, when he overthrew the cities in which Lot had settled.
>
> —*GENESIS 19:27–29*

Abraham saw smoke rising from the Plain, *keqitor hakkibsan*, like smoke jetting from a *kibsan*, a pottery kiln (Wood).

> That is what Abraham observed—smoke from the land of the plain being forced upwards. The word used for smoke, *qitor*, is not the word used for smoke from an ordinary fire. Rather, it is a thick smoke, the smoke that comes from sacrifices. It is clear that something unnatural or extraordinary is recorded here (Wood).

Smoke rising from the Plain below the Dead Sea would have been visible from Hebron. Abraham's description "fits the theory of a conflagration of petroleum products, for such a conflagration would result in a thick black smoke being forced into the sky by the heat and pressure of the burning materials shooting out of the fissure in the earth" (Wood).

This ends the Genesis 19 account of the destruction of the cities of the Plain. But we cannot form conclusions about the meaning of this account and the reason God overthew these cities from this passage alone, for Sodom, Gomorrah, and other cities are mentioned throughout the Bible in both the Old and New Testaments. Let's explore those passages and discover more.

11. Other Old Testament Passages Mentioning Sodom

The Bible testifies that the people of Sodom were "wicked, great sinners against the Lord" (Gen. 13:13). The Genesis 19 narrative includes the following crimes:

- Forcefulness
- Prejudice against outsiders
- Disrespect
- Cruelty
- Violence and physical abusiveness
- Intent to degrade, debase, humiliate, and dominate

It's no stretch to assert that the people of Sodom exemplified the antitheses of the fruit of the Spirit in Galatians 5:22–23.

In this chapter, we'll examine the remaining Old Testament passages concerning the cities of the Plain. So far we've covered all instances where *Sodom* is mentioned through the end of Genesis 19. Sodom and sometimes the other cities are mentioned in Deuteronomy, Isaiah, Jeremiah, Lamentations, Ezekiel, Amos, and Zephaniah.

Deuteronomy 29 and 32

In Deuteronomy 29, Moses gathers in the wilderness of Moab the entire community of Israel to renew the covenant (vv. 1,10–15). He recounts how they passed through the land of godless nations.

> [17]You have seen their detestable things, the *filthy idols* of wood and stone, of silver and gold, that were among them. [18]It may be that there is among you a man or woman, or a family or tribe, *whose heart is already turning away from the Lord our God to serve the gods of those nations.* It may be that there is among you a *root sprouting poisonous and bitter growth.*
>
> [19]All who hear the words of this oath and bless themselves, thinking in their hearts, "We are safe even though *we go our own stubborn ways*" (thus bringing disaster on moist and dry alike)— [20]the Lord will be unwilling to pardon them, for the Lord's anger and passion will smoke against them. All the curses written in this book will descend on them, and the Lord will blot out their names from under heaven. [21]The Lord will single them out from all the tribes of Israel for calamity, in accordance with all the curses of the covenant written in this book of the law.
>
> —*DEUTERONOMY 29:17–21*

Detestable practices, idolatry, apostasy, and spiritual adultery—all those things the people promised not to turn to— would bring on the curses of the law, which included calamity and the devastation of their Promised Land. Moses likens these attitudes and behaviors to a poisonous vine, which will crop up again in later passages. This is the context in which the cities of the Plain are next mentioned.

²²The next generation, your children who rise up after you, as well as the foreigner who comes from a distant country, will see the devastation of that land and the afflictions with which the Lord has afflicted it— ²³all its soil burned out by sulfur and salt, nothing planted, nothing sprouting, unable to support any vegetation, like the destruction of *Sodom and Gomorrah, Admah and Zeboiim,* which the Lord destroyed in his fierce anger— ²⁴they and indeed all the nations will wonder, "Why has the Lord done thus to this land? What caused this great display of anger?"

—*DEUTERONOMY 29:22-24*

The passage continues to reveal what would cause devastation like that visited upon the cities of the Plain:

²⁵They will conclude, "It is *because they abandoned the covenant of the Lord,* the God of their ancestors, which he made with them when he brought them out of the land of Egypt. ²⁶They *turned and served other gods, worshiping them,* gods whom they had not known and whom he had not allotted to them; ²⁷so the anger of the Lord was kindled against that land, bringing on it every curse written in this book. ²⁸The Lord uprooted them from their land in anger, fury, and great wrath, and cast them into another land, as is now the case."

—*DEUTERONOMY 29:25-28*

Moses next mentions Sodom and Gomorrah in his final song, in which he prophesies that the people of Jacob will abandon God, scoff the Rock of their salvation, follow after strange gods, and sacrifice to demons (Dt. 32:15-18). If God does not punish His people for their apostasy and wickedness, the heathen nations will mock Him.

[32]*Their vine comes from the vinestock of Sodom,*
  from the vineyards of Gomorrah;
their grapes are grapes of *poison,*
  their clusters are *bitter;*
[33]their wine is the poison of serpents,
  the cruel venom of asps.
[34]Is not this laid up in store with me,
  sealed up in my treasuries?
[35]Vengeance is mine, and recompense,
  for the time when their foot shall slip;
because the day of their calamity is at hand,
  their doom comes swiftly.
—DEUTERONOMY 32:32–35

The root of the word *vine* is "to bend or twist" (Strong's H1612), meaning to pervert or go astray. The "vine of Sodom" may refer to "the osher (*Calotropis procera*) of the Arabs, which grows from Jordan to southern Egypt. ... Its fruit are called 'apples of Sodom,' which, though beautiful to the eye, are bitter to the taste" (Vine of Sodom).

Calotropis procera is a species of flowering plant in the dogbane family.... The green globes are hollow but the flesh contains a toxic milky sap that is extremely bitter and turns into a gluey coating resistant to soap. ... The milky sap contains a complex mix of chemicals, some of which are steroidal heart poisons known as "cardiac aglycones." (Calotropis procera)

Jesus said that a plant is known by its fruit[44] and "every tree therefore that does not bear good fruit is cut down and thrown into the fire" (Mt. 3:10).

Israel's rebelliousness—and indeed the waywardness of all people—stems from the vinestock of Sodom. It cannot help but bear fruit that is bitter, poisonous to the heart, and so sticky that it refuses to be washed.

Deuteronomy 29:23 and 32:32 promise destruction like that which befell Sodom for those who *practice idolatry* and *abandon God's ways.*

Isaiah 1, 3, and 13

Isaiah's prophecy opens with a dark vision of Judah and Jerusalem.

> [4]Ah, sinful nation,
>   people laden with *iniquity,*
> offspring who *do evil,*
>   children who *deal corruptly,*
> who have *forsaken the Lord,*
>   who have *despised the Holy One of Israel,*
>   who are utterly estranged! …
>
> [7]Your country lies desolate,
>   your cities are burned with fire;
> in your very presence
>   aliens devour your land;
>   it is desolate, as overthrown by foreigners.
> [8]And daughter Zion is left
>   like a booth in a vineyard,

---

44 See Matthew 17:17–19; 12:33; Luke 3:9; 6:43.

like a shelter in a cucumber field,
  like a besieged city.
⁹If the Lord of hosts
  had not left us a few survivors,
we would have been like *Sodom*,
  and become like *Gomorrah*.
¹⁰*Hear the word of the Lord,*
  you rulers of Sodom!
Listen to the teaching of our God,
  you people of Gomorrah!
¹¹What to me is the multitude of your sacrifices?
  says the Lord;
I have had enough of burnt offerings of rams
  and the fat of fed beasts;
I do not delight in the blood of bulls,
  or of lambs, or of goats.
  —*ISAIAH 1:4,7–11*

The Lord speaks through Isaiah of His people's unfaithfulness, calling them "rulers of Sodom" and "people of Gomorrah." He denounces their incense and solemn assemblies and appointed festivals as hypocrisy.

¹⁵When you stretch out your hands,
  I will hide my eyes from you;
even though you make many prayers,
  I will not listen;
  your hands are full of blood.
¹⁶Wash yourselves; make yourselves clean;
  remove the evil of your doings
  from before my eyes;
cease to do evil,
¹⁷learn to do good;
seek justice,
  rescue the oppressed,

defend the orphan,
  plead for the widow.
—ISAIAH 1:15–17

Isaiah 1 compares Judah with Sodom and Gomorrah because of *iniquity, violence, bloodshed, evildoing,* and *oppression of the helpless.*

[8]For Jerusalem has stumbled
  and Judah has fallen,
because their speech and their deeds are against the Lord,
  defying his glorious presence.
[9]*The look on their faces* bears witness against them;
  they proclaim their sin like Sodom,
  they do not hide it.
Woe to them!
  For they have brought evil on themselves.
—ISAIAH 3:8–9

Jerusalem and Judah stumbled and fell because their speech and actions denied the Lord. The haughty look betrayed pride in flaunting their sin. This was a sin of Sodom. What does the Bible say of pride and haughtiness?

Haughty eyes and a proud heart—the lamp of the wicked—are *sin.*
—PROVERBS 21:4

For you deliver a humble people, but the haughty eyes you bring down.
—PSALM 18:27

Pride goes before destruction, and a haughty spirit before a fall.
—*PROVERBS 16:18*

In chapter 13, Isaiah prophesies against Babylon, who had overstepped their bounds in chastening God's people.

¹⁹And Babylon, the glory of kingdoms,
    the splendor and pride of the Chaldeans,
will be like *Sodom and Gomorrah*
    when God overthrew them.
²⁰It will never be inhabited
    or lived in for all generations;
—*ISAIAH 13:19–20a*

Isaiah 3:9 and 13:19 liken the sin of God's people and other nations to Sodom because of *pride in sinfulness.*

Jeremiah 23, 49, and 50

In chapter 23, Jeremiah denounces false shepherds who have scattered God's people. In verse 13, he decries the false prophets of Samaria, but then turns to the prophets of Jerusalem:

¹⁴But in the prophets of Jerusalem
    I have seen a more shocking thing:
they commit adultery and *walk in lies*;
    they strengthen the hands of evildoers,
    so that no one turns from wickedness;
*all of them have become like Sodom to me,
    and its inhabitants like Gomorrah.*
¹⁵Therefore thus says the Lord of hosts concerning the prophets:
"I am going to make them eat wormwood,
    and give them poisoned water to drink;

for *from the prophets of Jerusalem*
   ungodliness has spread throughout the land."
—*JEREMIAH 23:14–15*

Here, Jeremiah likens the prophets of Jerusalem and all of its people to that of Sodom and Gomorrah because they commit adultery, walk in lies, and strengthen the hands of evildoers, promoting ungodliness like a spreading vine throughout the land.

Jeremiah prophesies against Edom in chapter 49.

¹⁶The *terror you inspire*
   and *the pride of your heart* have deceived you,
you who live in the clefts of the rock,
   who hold the height of the hill.
Although you make your nest as high as the eagle's,
   from there I will bring you down,
says the Lord.
¹⁷Edom shall become an object of horror; everyone who passes by it will be horrified and will hiss because of all its disasters. ¹⁸As when *Sodom and Gomorrah* and their neighbors were overthrown, says the Lord, no one shall live there, nor shall anyone settle in it.

—*JEREMIAH 49:16–18*

Because the Edomites inspired terror and were proud in their hearts, the Lord promised to overthrow them and make their land desolate like the cities of the Plain. Likewise, he prophesied destruction for Babylon in chapter 50.

The Chaldeans were guilty of idolatry (50:2, 38), sinning against the Lord (v. 7), challenging the Lord (v. 24), defying the Lord (v. 29), and arrogance (vv. 31–32).

The prophetic message declares that a sword will be brought against "all the foreign troops in her midst, so that they may become women!" This is a reference to military domination and abasement of the enemy, as discussed previously in "Torture and Abuse at Abu Ghraib Prison" on page 55.

Because of these sins, what shall become of them?

> [39]Therefore wild animals shall live with hyenas in Babylon, and ostriches shall inhabit her; she shall never again be peopled, or inhabited for all generations. [40]*As when God overthrew Sodom and Gomorrah and their neighbors*, says the Lord, so no one shall live there, nor shall anyone settle in her.
> —*JEREMIAH 50:39–40*

Lamentations 4

Besides all of the wrongs delineated in his major book of prophecies, in Lamentations, Jeremiah lists against God's people a multitude of transgressions (1:5, 14, 22), grievous sin (1:8), uncleanness (1:9), rebelliousness (1:20), iniquity (2:14), and becoming cruel (4:3).

> [34]When all the prisoners of the land
>   are crushed under foot,
> [35]*WHEN HUMAN RIGHTS ARE PERVERTED*
>   *IN THE PRESENCE OF THE MOST HIGH,*
> [36]*when one's case is subverted*
>   —does the Lord not see it?
> —*LAMENTATIONS 3:34–36*

This passage states the prime reason judgment falls upon any people: *injustice that exploits human rights*. For these sins, Jeremiah says God's people have reaped a dire penalty:

> For the chastisement of my people has been greater
>   than the punishment of *Sodom*,
> which was overthrown in a moment,
>   though no hand was laid on it.

—*LAMENTATIONS 4:6*

Ezekiel 16

Ezekiel develops a decadent metaphor of Israelite apostasy in chapter 16. He speaks of abominations (vv. 2, 22, 43), whorings with heathen nations (vv. 15-17, 20, 24-26, 28-31, 33-36, 41), idolatry (vv. 17-19), sacrificing their children (vv. 20-21), wickedness (v. 23), lewd behavior (v. 27), spiritual adultery (v. 32, 38), lust (v. 36), and shedding blood (v. 38). Ezekiel includes Israel in the same family as Samaria and the cities of the Plain.

> 46Your elder sister is Samaria, who lived with her daughters to the north of you; and your younger sister, who lived to the south of you, is *Sodom* with her daughters. 47You not only followed their ways, and acted according to their abominations; within a very little time *you were more corrupt than they in all your ways.* 48As I live, says the Lord God, *your sister Sodom and her daughters have not done as you and your daughters have done.*

—*EZEKIEL 16:46-48*

Ezekiel indicts Israel with becoming more corrupt than Samaria and Sodom. What is the sin of Sodom he is referring to?

⁴⁹This was the guilt of your sister Sodom: she and her daughters had *pride, excess of food, and prosperous ease, but DID NOT AID THE POOR AND NEEDY.* ⁵⁰They were *haughty,* and *did abominable things*[45] before me; therefore I removed them when I saw it. ⁵¹Samaria has not committed half your sins; you have committed more abominations than they, and have made your sisters appear righteous by all the abominations that you have committed.

—*EZEKIEL 16:49–51*

This passage explicitly states that the sins of Sodom were arrogance and pride that led to being overfed (greedy and gluttonous), yet without concern for the poor and needy—a demonstration of complete selfishness and hardheartedness. These, in addition to all the crimes mentioned heretofore in this chapter, were the sins of Israel—greater than those of Samaria and the cities of the Plain combined.

[I]n 16.49–50 the evil of Sodom is clearly specified as *social injustice.* ... Here again we get an image of a rich and powerful society/class that oppresses the poor. Wealth has made them proud such that they do not try to hide their crimes. (Carden 47, emphasis mine).

Amos 4

Amos prophesied judgment and exile for God's people.

---

45 This is *tôebâ*, meaning "an abhorrence; especially idolatry" (Strong's H8441). It "occurs many times in the O.T. with regard to idolatry, often associated with the fertility cults of surrounding nations. This word is used in Lev. in a cultic context (not civil or criminal law – Ex. 20:22–23:3; Deut. 12–26)" (Horner 52).

After declaring judgments for the surrounding nations, he turns to Israel, declaring that God will strike them for their ruthless oppression and enslavement of the poor (2:6–7a); fathers and sons sexually using the same girl (2:7b–8); interfering with the Nazirites and prophets (2:11–13); oppression (3:9); wrongdoing, looting, hoarding plunder (3:10); idle luxury (3:12); oppressing the poor and crushing the needy, drunkenness (4:1); making sacrifices without turning from sin and then boasting about it (4:4–5).

For these crimes, the Lord brought hardship (4:6–10).

> I overthrew some of you,
> as when God overthrew *Sodom and Gomorrah*,
> and you were like a brand snatched from the fire;
> yet you did not return to me,
> says the Lord.
>
> —AMOS 4:11

Zephaniah 2

Zephaniah speaks of judgment and the coming day of the Lord. He denounces Judah for idolatry (1:4–9), complacency (1:12), and sinning against the Lord (1:17). Then he makes a pronouncement against Moab and Ammon who "insulted my people and made threats against their land" (2:8 NIV).

> ⁹Therefore, as I live, says the Lord of hosts,
> the God of Israel,
> Moab shall become like *Sodom*
> and the Ammonites like *Gomorrah*,
> a land possessed by nettles and salt pits,
> and a waste forever.

The remnant of my people shall plunder them,
   and the survivors of my nation shall possess them.
[10]*This shall be their lot in return for their pride,*
   because they scoffed and boasted
   against the people of the Lord of hosts.
—ZEPHANIAH 2:9–10

The sins of these surrounding nations—ironically the descendants from Lot's incest with his two daughters (see Genesis 19:36–38)—were pride, scoffing, and boasting.

A summary of Sodom's sins in the Old Testament

Although God likens his own wayward people to Sodom a number of times in the Old Testament, homosexuality is *not* mentioned as one of their crimes. This indicates that the prophets whom God inspired to pen the Scriptures did *not* see the sin of Sodom and Gomorrah as primarily a sexual one, let alone a homosexual one.

Isaiah rebuked Judah as a sinful nation, comparing it to the "rulers of Sodom" and the "people of Gomorrah" (Isa. 1:4, 10). The sins that Isaiah highlighted weren't sexual. *"They were sins of oppressing marginalized groups, murder, and theft."*

Jeremiah underscored the adultery, idolatry, and "power abuses of false prophets," which made them "all like Sodom" (Jer. 23:14). "Amos and Zephaniah, too, invoke Sodom to describe God's judgment on *those who 'oppress the poor' or exhibit prideful and mocking behavior* (Amos 4:1–11; Zephaniah 2:8–11)" (Vines 63, emphasis mine).

12. New Testament Passages Mentioning Sodom

In the New Testament, Sodom is mentioned in the gospels of Matthew and Luke. It is important to give attention to Jesus' view of the sin of Sodom. Remaining NT references are found in Romans, 2 Peter, Jude, and Revelation.

Matthew 10 and 11

Jesus has sent out the Twelve to the lost sheep of the house of Israel to preach the good news of the kingdom, heal the sick, and cast out demons. If they are received in peace, he says, they are to bless the household they stay at as sojourners. But,

> 14"If anyone will *not welcome* you or listen to your words, shake off the dust from your feet as you leave that house or town. 15Truly I tell you, it will be more tolerable for the land of *Sodom and Gomorrah* on the day of judgment than for that town."
> —MATTHEW 10:14–15

Jesus' message here is that those who reject God's visiting gospel messengers and *refuse them hospitality* will be judged harshly because the "sin of rejecting the Gospel merits greater punishment than the sin of Sodom and Gomorrah" (Jordan 32).

²⁰Then he began to reproach the cities in which most of his deeds of power had been done, because *they did not repent.* ²¹"Woe to you, Chorazin! Woe to you, Bethsaida! For if the deeds of power done in you had been done in Tyre and Sidon, they would have repented long ago in sackcloth and ashes. ²²But I tell you, on the day of judgment it will be more tolerable for Tyre and Sidon than for you. ²³And you, Capernaum, will you be exalted to heaven? No, you will be brought down to Hades. For if the deeds of power done in you had been done in *Sodom*, it would have remained until this day. ²⁴But I tell you that on the day of judgment it will be more tolerable for the land of *Sodom* than for you."

—*MATTHEW 11:20-24*

Christ himself traveled to these cities, preached the kingdom, and performed miracles there. But Chorazin, Bethsaida, and Capernaum rejected him and the delivering power of God.

Jesus condemns these cities because its inhabitants are *hardhearted and unrepentant.* Yet if the miracles that were done in Capernaum had been performed in Sodom, Sodom would have repented.

Here, as in the Old Testament, God's people are classed with the cities of the Plain and judged worse because of their behavior. "The parallel between the gospel and Sodom is the closed heart that rejects the stranger, the wickedness that will not welcome God's heralds" (Helminiak 49).

Luke 10 and 17

In Luke 10, Jesus sends out the seventy disciples on a mission to preach and demonstrate the kingdom. He says they must depend on the *hospitality* of the people they visit—hospitality like Abraham, Lot, and the old man at Gibeah showed wayfaring strangers.

> [5]"Whatever house you enter, first say, 'Peace to this house!' [6]And if anyone is there who shares in peace, your peace will rest on that person; but if not, it will return to you. [7]Remain in the same house, *eating and drinking whatever they provide*, for the laborer deserves to be paid. Do not move about from house to house. [8]Whenever you enter a town and *its people welcome you*, eat what is set before you; [9]cure the sick who are there, and say to them, 'The kingdom of God has come near to you.' [10]But *whenever you enter a town and they do not welcome you*, go out into its streets and say, [11]'Even the dust of your town that clings to our feet, we wipe off in protest against you. Yet know this: the kingdom of God has come near.' [12]I tell you, on that day it will be more tolerable for *Sodom* than for that town."
> —LUKE 10:5–12

Jesus says that when his messengers are *not welcomed* in a town, that town has committed the sin of Sodom. What is that sin? *Inhospitality!*

> The healing and the preaching of the kingdom are only offered in return for hospitality. Those towns that do not offer hospitality are not only ineligible to receive the gifts of the kingdom but have shown themselves to be like Sodom. Indeed these towns fare worse. Sodom did not welcome strangers, but these towns denied the emissaries of the coming kingdom of God. It could even be argued that, *without hospitality, the kingdom cannot come to be*. (Carden 50, emphasis mine)

Jesus understood the Old Testament Scriptures. He confirms what a straightforward study of the Genesis 19 passage reveals, which is in agreement with other Old Testament prophets.

Jesus never once mentioned homosexuality or any type of sexual sin as one of Sodom's crimes. He plainly indicates that the city's sins were hardheartedness, unrepentance, rejection of God's messengers, and lack of hospitality— disrespect, disdain, and mistreatment of outsiders and strangers.

Jesus taught his disciples about the coming of the kingdom and the final days of Jerusalem in Luke 17. He referred to Noah and to the events of Genesis 19.

> [28]"Likewise, just as it was in the days of Lot: they were eating and drinking, buying and selling, planting and building, [29]but on the day that Lot left *Sodom*, it rained fire and sulfur from heaven and destroyed all of them [30]—it will be like that on the day that the Son of Man is revealed. [31]On that day, anyone on the housetop who has belongings in the house must not come down to take them away; and likewise anyone in the field must not turn back. [32]Remember Lot's wife. [33]Those who try to make their life secure will lose it, but those who lose their life will keep it."
> —*LUKE 17:28-33*

Jesus refers to Lot, his wife, and the destruction of Sodom as a lesson to be ready, to take flight quickly and not look back. It's a lesson about the deliverance of the righteous when judgment comes on the ungodly.

Lot represents appropriate preparedness, being ready to let go of worldly things when he fled Sodom (Lk. 17.28–29). Lot's wife is used as a warning not to hold on to the ways of the world. (Carden 52)

Romans 9

In Romans 9 Paul discusses God's election of Israel, his wrath and his mercy. God chooses in mercy to deliver those apart from their merit.

> And as Isaiah predicted,
> "If the Lord of hosts had not left survivors to us,
>   we would have fared like *Sodom*
>   and been made like *Gomorrah*."
> —ROMANS 9:29

Without righteousness, destruction comes. Those who survive do so on the basis of faith in God's grace and mercy, something the cities of the Plain did not possess or practice.

2 Peter 2

Peter, in his second epistle, warns of false prophets, false teachers, and their judgment. He recalls the account of the fallen angels in the days of Noah.

> [4]For if God did not spare angels when they sinned, but sent them to hell, putting them in chains of darkness to be held for judgment; [5]if he did not spare the ancient world when he brought the flood on its ungodly people, but protected Noah, a preacher of righteousness, and seven others; [6]if he condemned the cities of *Sodom and Gomorrah* by burning them to ashes, and made them an *example* of what is going to happen to the *ungodly*; [7]and if he rescued Lot, a righteous

man, who was distressed by the *depraved conduct of the lawless* [8](for that righteous man, living among them day after day, was tormented in his righteous soul by the *lawless deeds* he saw and heard)— [9]if this is so, then the Lord knows how to rescue the godly from trials and to hold the unrighteous for punishment on the day of judgment. [10]This is especially true of those who follow the corrupt desire of the flesh and despise authority.

—*2 PETER 2:4–9 NIV*

Peter moves from the sin of angels in the day of Noah to the ungodliness, depravity, and lawlessness of Sodom and Gomorrah in the days of Lot. Although Lot is no shining star, the Apostle Peter presents him as an example of the fate of the righteous compared to the wicked.

What was Lot's redeeming feature? He showed hospitality to God's messengers on the eve of destruction.

Jude

Jude writes in defense of the gospel, warning his readers about ungodly false teachers infiltrating their midst.

[5]Now I desire to remind you, though you know all things once for all, that the Lord, after saving a people out of the land of Egypt, subsequently destroyed those who did not believe. [6]And *angels who did not keep their own domain*, but abandoned their proper abode, He has kept in eternal bonds under darkness for the judgment of the great day, [7]just as *Sodom and Gomorrah and the cities around them*, since they *in the same way as these indulged in gross immorality and went after strange flesh*, are exhibited as an example in undergoing the punishment of eternal fire.

—*JUDE 5–7 NASB*

Like Peter, Jude mentions that the angels of Noah's day exemplify the fate of false teachers. This deserves some examination.

Jude refers here to the angels of Genesis 6:1–2 who left their angelic estate to mate with human women. In the same way as these angels, the people of the Plain cities indulged in gross immorality and "went after strange flesh." This phrase in Greek is *heteros sarx*.

Many Christians see "strange flesh" here and equate it with the theory of homosexuality. But the context and the language tell us precisely what it means. *Heteros* means "strange, other, different" (Strong's G2087) and "denotes the new member of a series distinct from those which preceded, to introduce *another kind*" (Kittle, 2:702,265). From *heteros* we get the modern word *heterosexuality*.

There are several possible ways to view this going after *heteros* flesh. One not popularly known is: "The Jewish tradition to which Jude alludes was a legend that the *women* of Sodom had intercourse with the angels" (Boswell 97). In any case, it is definitely not homosexuality. "Far from arguing that the men of Sodom pursued flesh too similar to their own, Jude indicts them for pursing flesh that was too different" (Vines 69).

This passage refers not to homosexuality, but to the *violation of angels*, beings outside the natural human realm. The pseudoepigraphal work, *Testament of Naphtali*, found among the Dead Sea scrolls states, "[Be not] like Sodom, which changed the order of its nature. Likewise also the Watchers [angels of Noah's day] changed the order of their nature…" (3.3.4–5).

"Changed the order of nature" here refers not to male passion for other men, but "to the desire on the part of the men of Sodom to have sex with angels!" (Horner 53) This transgression earned the fallen angels of Noah's day bondage in the underworld (v. 6; 2 Pet. 2:4). In Lot's day, among the cities' many other crimes, it brought on fiery destruction.

Bribery is alluded to in verse 11, pointing to an economic component of their downfall, which agrees with Sodom's greed we have already determined from other biblical passages.

Revelation 11

Revelation chapter 11 speaks of the testimony of the two witnesses who are divinely protected until their testimony is complete.

> ⁷When they have finished their testimony, the beast that comes up out of the abyss will make war with them, and overcome them and kill them. ⁸And their dead bodies will lie in the street of the great city *which mystically is called Sodom and Egypt*, where also their Lord was crucified.
> —*REVELATION 11:7–8 NASB*

The two witnesses are killed in Jerusalem, where Jesus was crucified. It is called "Sodom and Egypt," indicating that the morals of the people of the "holy city" match that of those ancient peoples at their worst.

13. Sodom in Apocryphal Literature

Although Protestants exclude some inspired books from the canon of Scripture, these writings are nonetheless accepted by other branches of the Church, and they contain information about the cities of the Plain. We'll examine these passages in this chapter.

3 Maccabees 2

> [2]"Lord, Lord, king of the heavens and master of all creation, holy among the holy ones, only ruler, almighty: Pay attention to us. *We are being crushed by an evil and impure man, caught up in his own arrogance and power.* [3]You are the creator of all things and the just master who rules over all. *You judge those who act with violence and arrogance.* [4]You destroyed those who did evil in the past, even giants. The giants trusted in their bodily strength and boldness, but you destroyed them in a great flood. [5]*The people of Sodom acted arrogantly and were notorious for their wicked deeds.* You destroyed them with fire and sulfur, making them an example to others for all time.
>
> —3 MACCABEES 2:2–5 CEB

Simon the high priest prayed to the Lord, complaining that they were "being crushed by an evil and impure man, caught up in his own arrogance and power." He recounts that God judges those who act with violence and arrogance. Among those who do evil in this manner, the people of Sodom are mentioned, who "acted arrogantly and were notorious for their wicked deeds."

2 Esdras 2, 5, and 7

The writer of 2 Esdras begins the second chapter lamenting those who are unwilling to listen to the Lord and who ignore his advice. They have sinned and "done bad things in his sight" (2:3). He cites Assyria for disobedience.

> [8]How terrible it will be for you, Assyria—you who are *hiding the wicked in your midst*! Evil city, remember what I did to *Sodom and Gomorrah*, [9]whose land was dragged down all the way to hell. I will do the same to those who *haven't obeyed me*, says the almighty Lord.
>
> —*2 ESDRAS 2:8-9* CEB

2 Esdras 5:7 mentions Sodom in the context of apocalyptic judgment: "But about the signs: Look, the days will come when those who live on earth will be seized with great terror. The way of truth will be hidden, and the land will be barren and devoid of faith" (CEB). One of these signs is that "The sea of Sodom will cast up fish; it will utter sounds in a voice that many don't know, but all will hear its voice" (CEB).

The sea of Sodom, according to Jewish writers, is "'the salt sea,' as 'the bituminous sea,'" referring to the Dead Sea. The Talmud devotes to the sea of Sodom anything destined to "rejection and cursing, and that by no means is to be used" (Lightfoot).

In 2 Esdras 7, an angel is speaking to Ezra about a decisive day of judgment. Ezra says: "How then do we find that

Abraham first interceded for the people of Sodom; and Moses for our ancestors who sinned in the desert" (7:106 CEB).

The angel replies that "the Judgment Day will be the end of this time and the beginning of the future, endless time in which decay is no more, indulgence is undone, unbelief is cut off, but justice is fully grown, and truth arisen" (7:113–114 CEB).

Like the fate of Sodom, the final judgment will be without recourse. The mention of Sodom here connects the people's sins with sexual immorality connected with idolatry in both the time of Abraham and Moses.

Sirach 16

⁶A fire will be kindled
in an assembly of sinners,
   and wrath will flash forth
   in a *disobedient nation.*
⁷The Lord didn't seek reconciliation
with the ancient giants
   who *rebelled in their might.*
⁸He didn't spare Lot's neighbors,
   whom he detested
   because of their *arrogance.*

—*SIRACH 16:8 CEB*

This passage describes God's fiery judgment on the disobedient. The Lord did not show mercy to the giants—the offspring of the angels of God who mated with human woman (Gen. 6). Likewise, he abhorred the people of Sodom and the other cities of the Plain because of their pride and arrogance. Sexual sin is not mentioned.

So while both stories in Genesis contain a sexual element, it plays no part in linking them together in either Sirach or 3 Maccabees. ... [N]either Sirach nor 3 Maccabees use the stories to exemplify sexual misconduct (Carden 48).

Wisdom 18 and 19

Wisdom chapters 18 and 19 recount Israel's deliverance from Egypt and contrasts the overthrow of the ungodly.

> [13]In contrast, punishments rained down upon the sinners, but not before they were given a clear warning through violent thunder. *It was right for them to suffer for their evil deeds and for their hatred of the immigrants in their midst.* [14]*Some people have failed to welcome strangers who came into their midst to stay awhile. But these people went so far as to make slaves of people who were their guests and benefactors.* [15]Judgment will come on those who *greeted people who weren't like them as enemies.* [16]But these people first gave feasts to welcome those who did right and shared with them the blessings of the land. But then they began to *force the strangers to do hard labor.* [17]Therefore, *they were struck blind, just like those people who had gathered at the door of one who had also done what was right.* A veil of darkness was cast around them, and each one of them groped for the entrance to his own gates.
>
> —*WISDOM 19:13–17* CEB

This passage is quite telling in its analysis of the sin of Sodom and those societies like it. The writer highlights the following crimes:

- Failing to welcome sojourning strangers
- Making guests and benefactors slaves

- Treating people unlike themselves as enemies
- Forcing strangers to do hard labor

For the author of Wisdom, Sodom is clearly not associated with sexual sin. Instead, like Egypt of the Exodus, Sodom is a place of injustice and oppression. This oppression is portrayed as a form of inhospitality of which the paragon is Sodom. (Carden 49)

For these sins, they were struck blind.

Being blinded in Scripture

There are several incidences of people being struck blind in Scripture. "In each and every case in the Bible of people being struck blind there was an action or actions of gross rebellion against God or the people of God (or both)" (Blinded). We see this happening with God's people in Isaiah 59.

> [10]Like the *blind* we grope along the wall,
>   feeling our way like people without eyes.
> At midday we stumble as if it were twilight;
>   among the strong, we are like the dead. ...
> [12]For our *offenses* are many in your sight,
>   and our *sins* testify against us.
> Our *offenses* are ever with us,
>   and we acknowledge our *iniquities*:
> [13]*rebellion and treachery against the Lord,*
>   *turning our backs on our God,*
> *inciting revolt and oppression,*
>   *uttering lies our hearts have conceived.*
> [14]So *justice* is driven back,
>   and *righteousness* stands at a distance;[46]

truth has stumbled in the streets,
    honesty cannot enter.
[15]Truth is nowhere to be found,
    and *whoever shuns evil becomes a prey.*
The Lord looked and was displeased
    that there was no justice.
—ISAIAH 59:10,12–15 NIV

All such people who turn their backs on God and exalt wickedness and suppress righteousness will be stricken blind as the angels did to the people of Sodom who gathered at Lot's front door.

---

46 Here is a prime example of the values of righteousness and justice being paired and contrasted with the sins of those like the people of Sodom. For more information, see "What have we learned so far?" on page 36.

14. Summary of the Biblical Sins of Sodom

In all of the biblical passages, we find the following sins and crimes delineated:

Book	Sins akin to Sodom's
Genesis	Wickedness and sin Inhospitality Forcefulness Prejudice against outsiders Disrespect Cruelty Violence and physical/sexual abusiveness Intent to degrade, debase, dominate and humiliate
Deuteronomy	Detestable practices Idolatry Apostasy Spiritual adultery Abandoning God Scoffing the Rock of their salvation Following after strange gods Sacrificing to demons

Book	Sins akin to Sodom's
Isaiah	Unfaithfulness Hypocrisy Iniquity Violence Bloodshed Evildoing Oppressing the helpless Haughtiness Pride in sinfulness
Jeremiah	Adultery Walking in lies Strengthening the hands of evildoers Promoting ungodliness Inspiring terror Pride Idolatry Sinning against the Lord Challenging the Lord Defying the Lord Arrogance
Lamentations	Transgressions Grievous sin Uncleanness Rebelliousness Iniquity Becoming cruel Injustice that exploits human rights

Book	Sins akin to Sodom's
Ezekiel	Abominations Whorings with heathen nations Idolatry Child sacrifice Wickedness Lewd behavior Spiritual adultery Lust Shedding blood Pride Greed Gluttony No concern for the poor and needy
Amos	Ruthless oppression and enslavement of the poor Fathers and sons sexually using the same girl Interfering with the Nazirites and prophets Oppression Wrongdoing, looting, hoarding plunder Idle luxury Oppressing the poor and crushing the needy Drunkenness Making sacrifices without turning from sin and then boasting about it

Book	Sins akin to Sodom's
Zephaniah	Idolatry Complacency Sinning against the Lord Pride Scoffing Boasting
Matthew	Hardheartedness Unrepentance
Luke	Inhospitality
Romans	Unbelief
2 Peter	Ungodliness Depravity Lawlessness
Jude	Gross immorality Going after "strange flesh" (angelic)— violating God's created order
Revelation	Rejecting God's messengers
3 Maccabees	Violence Arrogance Wicked deeds
2 Esdras	Ignoring the Lord and his advice Disobedience Idolatry Sexual immorality

Book	Sins akin to Sodom's
Sirach	Disobedience Rebellion Pride Arrogance
Wisdom	Failing to welcome sojourning strangers Making guests and benefactors slaves Treating people unlike themselves as enemies Forcing strangers to do hard labor

The chief sins are *inhospitality, idolatry, hatred of strangers, and abuses against human rights.* Sexual sins are in the minority, most are metaphorical of spiritual adultery, and homosexuality is not mentioned. Instead, pride and arrogance are primary.

15. Historical Views About the Sin of Sodom and Gomorrah

We have examined every mention of Sodom in Scripture. But our investigation is not complete. Other ancient and historical writings about the cities of the Plain provide perspectives that confirm the biblical account—or depart from it. We'll consider them in this chapter.

Evangelical writer Matthew Vines asks the important question, "Does Scripture teach that Sodom and Gomorrah were destroyed because of God's wrath against same-sex relations? And if not, how have so many people come to believe that for so long?" (Vines 60)

The tabulation of Sodom's sins in "Summary of the Biblical Sins of Sodom" on page 113 lists everything but homosexuality. How did the present-day Church arrive at this interpretation, if not through careful study of the Scriptures? Let's review history.

Philo's view

Scholar Michael Carden identifies the Hellenistic Jewish philosopher Philo of Alexandria (ca. 25 B.C. – ca. A.D. 50), who lived in Alexandria, a Roman province of Egypt, as the first to interpret the Hebrew word *yada* ("to know") with a homosexual connotation. In fact, Carden considers "Philo to

be the inventor of the homophobic reading of Genesis 19"
(Carden 61).

> Outside of Philo, the dominant pattern focuses on Sodom's
> injustice, lawlessness and hostility to outsiders as the primary
> evils leading to divine intervention. Hatred of strangers
> figures along with pride and impiety as the crimes that make
> the deity decide to destroy Sodom in Josephus' account. (77)

Philo compares same-sex behavior to gluttony and drunkenness (Vines 70), through which men pursue other men while
also following their lust for women:

> Incapable of bearing such satiety, plunging like cattle, they
> threw off from their necks the law of nature and applied
> themselves to deep drinking of strong liquor and dainty feed-
> ing and forbidden forms of intercourse. Not only in their
> mad lust for women did they violate the marriages of their
> neighbours, but also men mounted males without respect for
> the sex nature which the active partner shares with the
> passive; and so when they tried to beget children they were
> discovered to be incapable of any but a sterile seed. (Philo)

Philo's understanding in his day, then, was that men
pursued men *in addition to* their "mad lust for women." The
crime was for a male to be the passive (receptive) partner,
degrading because it made him like a woman.

Jewish views of Sodom

The *Talmud* (meaning "instruction" or "learning") is a central
text of Rabbinic Judaism that expounds broadly on the
Hebrew Scriptures and "contains the teachings and opinions

of thousands of pre-Christian Era rabbis on a variety of subjects" (Talmud). It reveals a Hebraic understanding of the
account of Sodom and Gomorrah prior to the Christian era.
Carden states:

> Sodom and Gomorrah are sites of covetous greed and
> arrogance. ... Rapacious, abusive and greedy, the people of
> Sodom and Gomorrah know nothing of the heavenly ways of
> hospitality. ... Sodom in the *Talmud* is very much a byword
> for *'dog in the manger' attitudes, smugness, selfishness and
> generally vexatious behaviour* (*Erubin* 49a, *Kethuboth* 103a,
> *Baba Bathra* 12a, 59a, 168a, *Aboth* V.10). It is not, as
> Christians might expect, a name connoting sexual difference
> or sexual sin. ...

He further states:

> Their crimes are portrayed as *exploitation of the poor and
> abuse of strangers combined with the corruption of justice to
> favour the rich and powerful.* The Sodomites are haughty and,
> because their land is rich and they are well provided for, they
> resolve, 'why should we suffer wayfarers, who come to us
> only to deplete our wealth... let us abolish the practice of
> travelling in our land' (*Sanh.* 109a). Wealthy travellers are
> particularly targeted and subjected to violence, even being
> killed, so that their wealth can be stolen. The poor, on the
> other hand, are mistreated, and denied any aid or assistance
> so that they starve in the midst of a wealthy city. One particu-
> lar cruelty depicted is a bed on which strangers are made to
> lie –'(i)f he (the guest) was too long, they shortened him (by
> lopping off his feet); if too short, they stretched him out'
> (*Sanh.* 109b). No reason is given for such behaviour. It

represents a particularly gratuitous form of cruelty on the part of the Sodomites. (Carden 94–95, emphasis mine)

Carden summarizes the *Talmud*'s view of Sodom:

The system of justice in Sodom and its fellow cities is designed to oppress every stranger passing through, to fleece them of everything so that, if they are lucky enough to leave, they leave literally naked. (97)

Nowhere does the *Sefer ha-Yashar* (the *Book of Jasher*, mentioned in Joshua 10:13 and 2 Samuel 1:18) "associate homoeroticism with Sodom." Instead, says Carden, "heterosexual adultery and wife-swapping serve to typify Sodom's sexual excesses" (99).

Classical Jewish texts major on the aspect of Sodom's inhospitality and cruelty to strangers. The *Jewish Encyclopedia* states,

In Sodom every one who gave bread and water to the poor was condemned to death by fire (*Yalk.*, Gen. 83). Two girls, one poor and the other rich, went to a well; and the former gave the latter her jug of water, receiving in return a vessel containing bread. When this became known, both were burned alive (ib.). (Jacobs and Ochser)

Rabbinic writings reveal that the people of Sodom were guilty of economic crimes, bloodshed, and blasphemy (Loader 28). "One of the worst was to give money or even gold ingots to beggars, after inscribing their names on them, and then subsequently refusing to sell them food. The unfortunate stranger would end up starving and after his death, the people who gave him the money would reclaim it" (Sodom: Wikipedia).

It seems that the citizens of these cities made a sport of cruelty and debasement. The following quotation sets the tone for their practices:

> The *Talmud* and the *Sefer haYashar* (midrash) also recount two incidents of a young girl (one involved Lot's daughter Paltith) who gave some bread to a poor man who had entered the city. When the townspeople discovered their acts of kindness, they burned Paltith and smeared the other girl's body with honey and hung her from the city wall until she was eaten by bees. (*Sanhedrin* 109a.) It is this gruesome event, and her scream in particular, the *Talmud* concludes, that are alluded to in the verse that heralds the city's destruction: "So said, 'Because the outcry of Sodom and Gomorrah has become great, and because their sin has been very grave, I will descend and see...'" (Gen. 18:20–21). (Sodom: Wikipedia)

Carden claims that the people of Sodom "are not just thieves or gangsters but take special delight in vexatious harassment of their victims" (Carden 100).

Spanish rabbis Ramban (Moshe ben Nachman, 1194–1274) and Arama (Yitzchak ben Moshe Arama, 1420–1494) have written that Sodom's society "represents structured injustice. Sodom is not just a city of individuals who collectively share a taste for evil, but rather the whole society has been structured so as to maintain evil" (101–102).

> It is this inability to give, share or extend help to others that Arama sees as intrinsic to Sodomite society. *Sodom passed*

laws designed to prevent help being given to the weak and the outsider. If 'someone were to… extend help to outsiders, he would be in defiance of their laws and face death, even if it involved offering benefits to a third party at no cost or inconvenience to the donor' (Arama 1986: 146). *Sodom's laws were designed to 'frighten off would be visitors, and ensure an UNDISTURBED life for its inhabitants'* (Arama 1986:147). Citing *Genesis Rabbah*, Arama argues that *the Sodomites had resolved to rape and rob every stranger to give their city the evil reputation and deter travellers coming there.* (102, emphasis mine)

What, then, are Sodom's crimes warranting complete destruction?

[S]exual misdeeds alone, such as the Sodomites threatened upon Lot's guests, do not constitute an evil warranting divine intervention in Sodom. *It is Sodom's sanctioned use of violence including sexual violence to maintain a cruel, oppressive and selfish social system that incurs the divine wrath.* (103, emphasis mine)

The Jewish-Roman historian Flavius Josephus writes, "[T]he Sodomites grew proud, on account of their riches and great wealth; *they became unjust towards men, and impious towards God*, insomuch that they did not call to mind the advantages they received from him: *they hated strangers*, and abused themselves with Sodomitical practices" (Josephus Antiq. 1.11.1, emphasis mine). Although it is uncertain what Josephus means by "Sodomitical practices," it probably refers to their sexual sin of humiliation of strangers by gang rape.

Note that the sin of Sodom's citizens is principally that they *hated and abused strangers*. As pointed out in a previous chapter, their sexual sin was only a *means* of demeaning outsiders, like the soldiers at Abu Ghraib Prison (page 55).

"In the Jewish tradition," Carden concludes, "Sodom's crime is constantly associated with *oppression, injustice, greed and hostility toward strangers*" (113, emphasis mine).

How interpretation changed in the Christian era

Carden states that "Judaism understood Sodom's crime to be inhospitality and abuse of outsiders." Early Christians originally shared this understanding. (Carden 128) But this perspective began to change within a few years after the advent of Christ.

Tertullian, Origen and Basil

Early church writer Tertullian (ca. A.D. 155 – ca. 240) cites the story of Lot's wife in condemnation of remarriage, the only topic that hints of sexual sin.

Origen (ca. 184 – 254) does not pursue sexual themes in his reading. He sees Sodom only as "a place of general injustice," indicating that Lot is saved because of his practice of hospitality (132).

Basil the Great (ca. 329 – 379) sees not homoeroticism but gluttony as Sodom's primary sin.

Jerome and Amandus

Jerome (ca. 347 – 420) "declares that the first sin of Sodom and her daughters is pride, the primary sin of the devil (*Comm. Hiez.* 5.16.48–51)" (139). "The Sodomitic sin is pride, bloatedness, the abundance of all things, leisure and delicacies (*Comm. Hiez.* 5.16.48–51).” Jerome does not mention or condemn same-sex desire in the Genesis 19 account (139). Rather, “the sin of Sodom is brazen arrogance bred of opulence” (Jordan 33).

It was Amandus (ca. 584 – 675) who first coined the word *sodomite* in an A.D. 395 letter to Jerome. But the term is not defined and its meaning is unknown.

Nilus of Sinai demonstrated that the word *sodomite* could be used with no specific sexual meaning intended (Carden 139). The word actually means an inhabitant of the city of Sodom, just as natives of Chicago are called *Chicagoans*.

John Chrysostom

The first Christian to attribute same-sex desire and homoeroticism to the biblical Sodom account is John Chrysostom (ca. 349 – 407), Archbishop of Constantinople.

> His commentary on the story, in his Homilies 41–44 on Genesis, specifically attempts to blend a homophobic reading of the story with the more traditional emphasis on inhospitality and rejection of outsiders as the sins of Sodom. Chrysostom seems to suggest that such hatred of fellow humans is a natural result of surrendering to same-sex desire. (141)

Chrysostom seems to have put the cart full of wickedness before the horse. Instead of same-sex desire leading to mistreatment of outsiders, as he posits, it is inhospitality and the hatred of strangers that led the people of Sodom to treat sojourners in the basest of ways.

Since both the cities of the Plain and the citizens of Gibeah held these dark values and practices, they treated visitors with violence to the point of rape and murder. As we have seen, their atrocious actions had nothing to do with same-sex desire, but everything to do with xenophobic cruelty. Rape, whether homosexual or heterosexual, was only the means of expressing their dominance and exploitation.

Commenting on Romans 1:26–27, Chrysostom reminds his readers of Sodom's fate as a warning to those who engage in homosexual behavior.

> In *Against the Opponents of the Monastic Life*, he denounces same-sex desire as a 'new and lawless lust… a terrible and incurable disease… a plague more terrible… a great abomination' (*Adv. Oppugn.* 3.8). He warns that those 'who dare to commit the sins of Sodom' and have not learned from Sodom's fate are 'worthy of a greater punishment' (*Adv. Oppugn.* 3.8). (142)

Chrysostom still has the cart before the horse here, for Romans 1:18–32 explains that being given over to sexual perversion is the eventual *result* of idolatry.[47] In spite of this misunderstanding, "Chrysostom still defers to the priority of hospitality and the right treatment of outsiders as the issues central to the story of Sodom" (144).

---

47 For an incisive examination of this passage from a Reformed evangelical perspective, see James V. Brownson, *Bible, Gender, Sexuality: Reframing the Church's Debate on Same-Sex Relationships.* Grand Rapids, MI: William B. Eerdmans Publishing Company, 2013. Print. ISBN 0802868630.

Ambrose and Cassian

Ambrose (ca. 340 – 397), bishop of Milan, also sees same-sex desire as Sodom's crime, attempting "to graft homophobia onto inhospitality" (146).

> In Ambrose the moral sense of Sodom begins to narrow around sexual or at least bodily sin. He does recognize that the threat against the angels was a violation of hospitality. Elsewhere, … he identifies Sodom straightforwardly with fleshly indulgence and lasciviousness. (Jordan 34)

John Cassian (ca. 360 – ca. 435) held that Sodom's sin was gluttony, but that "overeating caused the people to become 'inflamed with uncontrollable lust of the flesh'" (Vines 72).

Augustine and Gregory

"There can be little doubt," says Carden, "that Augustine considers same-sex desire and homoeroticism to be the main evil of Sodom and Gomorrah" (Carden 146).

Augustine (354 – 430) "is quite clear that the citizens of Sodom wanted to rape the male angels" (Jordan 34). Augustine had a problem with all kinds of sex, however, and believed that even all non-procreative heterosexual relations within the bounds of marriage were evil.

"Sexual desire," he says, "must be constantly controlled, otherwise it will lead humans into the homoerotic chaos of Sodom, which for Augustine, incurred the divine punishment" (Carden 147).

> With Augustine, then, we reach an explicit description of the sin of the Sodomites as the desire for same-sex copulation. …

But even in Augustine the sin of the Sodomites is not merely same-sex desire. That desire is a symptom of the madness of their fleshly appetites, of the underlying delirium of their passions. The root sin of the Sodomites is... the violent eruption of disordered desire itself. (Jordan 35)

Augustine believed it was better for women to be violated than men: "The body of a man is as superior to that of a woman as the soul is to be body" (De Mend. 7.10).

Carden sums up the developments of the early Christian era:

The homophobic interpretation becomes established by the end of the fourth century, though Jerome adheres to the older interpretation. To John Chrysostom belongs the credit for systematically developing the homophobic reading by grafting it onto the established reading so that inhospitality is replaced by homoeroticism as the main sin of Sodom. ... He is followed in this enterprise by the Western Fathers, Ambrose and Augustine. The latter prefers the homophobic reading as most suited to his own theology of sexuality and marriage, thus entrenching the homophobic interpretation in the Latin West. (Carden 154)

Pope Gregory the Great (ca. 540 – 604) understood Ezekiel's treatment of Sodom (see page 95). But his main thought "is of sexual sin, not of pride or inhospitality" (Jordan 35).

The passages from Gregory make two things clear. The first is that *Latin exegesis had by the end of the patristic period fixed on a sexual interpretation of Sodomitic sin*, even if it kept repeating the other interpretations offered by the Scriptures. ... The misreading of Sodom has intersected with the formation of Christian moral categorizations in the Latin-speaking West. (37, emphasis mine)

The Eastern understanding

In the Syrian East, however, Christian writers did not see the sin of Sodom as out-of-control sexual desire, but "arrogant disdain for the rest of humanity" (Carden 151).

The word *sodomite* in this tradition refers to an evil shared by Sodom and Gibeah: "cruel delight in victimizing others, including sexual violence directed at men and women alike" (160).

Misogyny key to interpretation

What do these early Church writers have to say about the Judges 19 Gibeah account? Nearly all of them ignore it (Carden 160). Why? Could it be because the crime in Gibeah was ultimately against a woman?

> [T]he worst troubles linked to condemnations of Sodomy have to do with misogyny. It is hard to find a single condemnation in the theological tradition that does not rely on misogynistic logic. They condemn violently anything feminine, but especially anything that seems to surrender masculine privilege. ... They depend on the familiar male horror about women. Within this horror, to be a woman is to be something defective, something already half-polluted, something disreputable. But this horror is surely not something that Christian theology ought to permit, much less endorse. ... The forces that power extreme condemnations of Sodomy seem also to produce condemnations of the unclean, the ignoble, and the feminine. Each of these condemnations ought to be suspect for a Christian. (Jordan 169)

Misogyny is the key to comprehending the threat of homophobic violence in both the Genesis and Judges accounts. For a man to be penetrated by another man is to make him a woman, of less value and acceptable to be sacrificed like Lot's daughters or the Levite's concubine to sexual abuse and death.

Those who continue the homophobic interpretation of Sodom's sin in essence continue to celebrate the deprecation of women.

Paul of Hungary

Paul of Hungary wrote a *Summa of Penance* about 1220 after the Fourth Lateran Council to summarize and apply the council's decisions on regular confessions. The *Summa* is divided into two parts: the first treats the practice of confession; the second synopsizes the principal vices and virtues.

Following Gregory's classification, the vices are divided according to the seven capital sins: vainglory, anger, envy, sloth, avarice, gluttony, and *luxury*—a broad category for sexual immorality. These are further subdivided each into categories, one of which is the "sin against nature." This final section makes up about forty percent of the entire document and became a freestanding work. In it, he names the "sin against nature" as sodomy, which includes any type of sexual activity outside of non-procreative vaginal sex (Jordan 93–94).

Paul of Hungary interpreted incorrectly that the epistle of Jude is referring to male-male and female-female sex in going after "strange flesh"—not the flesh of angels as is clearly taught in the Scriptures (see "Jude" on page 104). Paul writes:

Sodomites are the adversaries of God, and murderers and destroyers of humankind. They seem to say to God, "You created human beings to multiply. But we work so that your work may be destroyed." (Summa, 208b–209a)

According to Paul of Hungary, sodomy was a capital offense (Jordan 101).

Peter Damian

By the time of the medieval Church, through the work of a Benedictine monk and cardinal, Peter Damian (ca. 1007 – ca. 1073), the word *sodomy* had been coined as a purely homophobic term. Damian writes: "If blasphemy (*blasphemia*) is the worst sin, I do not know in what way sodomy (*sodomia*) is any better" (Damian, *Liber Gomorrhianus* [Reindel 328.2–3]). "*Blasphemia, sodomia.* ... The sameness links those who perform them back to the criminals who suffered the most severe divine punishment" (Jordan 43).

Damian's *Book of Gomorrah*, a work against clerical homosexuality, was addressed to Pope Leo IX around A.D. 1050. In it, Damian refers to the "Sodomitic vice," the "Sodomitic manner" of copulation, and coins the first use of the word *sodomy* (46).

Damian clearly "equated Sodom with all expressions of same-sex desire," including masturbation (Carden 176). In this persuasive treatise, Damian waged an early battle "against a 'vice' and a 'hot disgrace'" that he calls "'most wicked' and 'most shameful.'" The document's obscenity prompted later editors to censor it (Jordan 45).

The booklet begins by identifying the vice's four species: self-pollution, mutual grasping or rubbing of "manly parts" (*virilia*), pollution "between the thighs" (*inter femora*), and fornication "in the rear" (*in terga*). The order of these four is an order of increasing offense, but each belongs to Sodom and each merits suspension from ecclesiastical office and deposition from priestly orders. (46)

Damian argues, "It is better for a community to be without a priest—or the church without a pope—than to be served by a Sodomite." Damian wanted to convince the pope to "suppress vice by punishing those who practice it" through penance and removal from "clerical status and ecclesiastical office" (47–48).

Although addressed to the pope, Damian knew the booklet would be read by monks and priests. At the crisis of his thesis Damian addresses these ecclesiastical inhabitants of Sodom: "Now I come face to face with you, Sodomite, whoever you are." The document was cleverly written "as a therapeutic address to the concealed Sodomite [the cleric in the "closet"], who must be persuaded without being identified, since he must be persuaded to identify himself. The booklet aims to produce self-judgment" (48–49).

According to Jordan, "Peter Damian fears a church of Sodom with the church of God" (50), a theme I will return to in the conclusion of this book. He eventually classes sodomites with demoniacs; they are the "prey of demons" (55).

Finally, he addresses these sodomites "with the full force of scriptural condemnation: the horror of divine fire at Sodom, the executions prescribed by Leviticus, the trumpet call of Paul's excoriation in Romans." For the guilty, Damian reads the penalty literally: death (55).

What is the ultimate result of his treatment of this greatest sin?

> Peter Damian has also built into his coinage of the category "Sodomy" one of the fundamental paradoxes that will trouble its theological history. *He seems to conceive Sodomy as a sin that cannot be repented.* This conception violates the fundamental Christian teaching about sins of the flesh, namely, that they are always repentable. (65–66)

If there is a sin of the flesh that cannot be repented of, it denies there is sanctification in the Christian walk (see 1Th. 4:2–3). What good is there, then, of repentance in the first place?

Peter Cantor

French theologian Peter Cantor (d. 1197) wrote a commentary on Genesis 18–19 titled *De Vitio Sodomitico—The Sodomitic Vice*. In it, he applies the term to both male-male and female-female same-sex desire (Carden 180). For Cantor,

> There are only two sins whose gravity calls out to heaven, murder and the sodomitic vice (*PL* 205: 334A). ... Such desire resembles murder because it repudiates divinely sanctioned reproductive sexuality. (160)

Cantor also cited Church regulations that hermaphrodites must choose which sex organ they will use and never use the other. If they ever use the rejected organ, the hermaphrodite is guilty of the "sodomitic vice" (182).

During roughly the same time period, more moral treatises were written that dealt with sexual sin in detail, including Robert of Flamborough's *Penitential Book* (ca. 1210), Peter of

Poitier's *Compilation*, the writings of Robert of Sorbonne, William of Auxerres/Peter Chanter's *Book of Cases of Conscience*, Raymund of Peñafort's *Summa*, and William Peraldus' *Summa of the Vices and the Virtues*.

Thomas Aquinas

Dominican theologian Thomas Aquinas (1225 – 1274) stopped writing his "greatest achievement in morals," the *Summa of Theology* about 1273; he never finished it. Although many summas were authored in the thirteenth century, Aquinas's work exceeds them "in simplicity, scope, and rigor of organization" (Jordan 140). By the 1500s it had become the leading authority, displacing Peter Lombard's *Sentences*, which it drew heavily from. It became a primary text in university theology departments (136).

Every summa covers a broad range of subjects under the headings of virtues and vices. The subject of sodomy appears in only two questions about others concerning the vice of *luxuria* (2–2.153–154).

Luxuria, according to Aquinas, is a vice of excess in "venereal pleasures"[48] and is applied not only to sexual immoralities but the "self-indulgent excesses such as drinking too much wine" (143). Aquinas divides the broad category of *luxuria* into six kinds: "simple fornication, adultery, incest, deflowering, abduction, and vice against nature" (144).

The "vice against nature" includes, in order of gravity, being polluted ("pollution" = seminal emission) without

---

48 Meaning "of or relating to sexual pleasure or indulgence," "inclined to be lascivious."

sleeping with another (involving only oneself), "doing so by sleeping with a member of another species, doing so by sleeping with someone not of the proper sex, and doing so in other than the natural way, either by using an improper instrument or by using certain 'monstrous and bestial manners' (154.11 corp)" (144). Of these vices against nature, "the worst is bestiality, the least serious, solitary uncleanness (154.12 ad 4)" (145).

Although the sodomitic vice is not the most severe, Aquinas clearly understood "that same-sex desire and homoeroticism are the defining sins of Sodom" (183).

Synopsizing writings by Aristotle, Aquinas connects "cannibalism, bestiality, and same-sex copulation under the notion of bestial desire." He also continues the tradition among contemporary writers that considers the vice against nature to be the "vice that cannot be named," doing so according to a misunderstanding of Ephesians 5:3 (150). Theologians who followed Aquinas continue to misread his writing, compiling misunderstandings about the vice against nature.

We must remember that our modern understandings of sexual orientation and gender issues cannot be retrofitted into thirteenth-century theology. In fact, the broad category of sexuality is a "fairly recent invention" (156). Jordan reminds us:

[T]here is nothing resembling the categories "homosexual" and "heterosexual" in Thomas [Aquinas]. Thomas cannot responsibly be made to even speak in debates where homosexuality and heterosexuality serve as categories for personal identity. When Thomas talks about the sodomitic vice, he is talking about a vice. The vice is precisely not a physiological disposition or its behavioral consequences. Neither is it an identity determining the whole of a person's actions. Nor does the vice have anything specifically to do with gender inversions or exaggerations. Indeed, ...there are no references to gender at all in Thomas's passages on same-sex copulation. (155, emphasis mine)

This means that same-sex activity was only *activity*; it did not determine anyone's *identity*. In other words, we cannot use Aquinas's ideas or language to support lumping all people having same-sex orientation into a category that we bind up and cast into hell. But this is what has been done, especially in the Western Church.

Summary

We see that from the fourth century through the thirteenth, the sin of Sodom morphed from its historical understanding of pride, arrogance, and inhospitality into same-sex desire, whose proper punishment was "genocidal mass murder" (193). What disappeared from interpretation of the Genesis 19 account is its obvious connection to Judges 19 and the crimes of Gibeah.

Medieval Church theology departed from the statements of Scripture. Once having changed the meaning of the sin of Sodom from inhospitality and pride to same-sex coupling, interpretive theology continued to pile atop it until a monstrous misunderstanding resulted that has for hundreds of years tormented, condemned, and harmed millions of people.

To paraphrase Genesis 18:20–21: "How great is the outcry against ~~Sodom and Gomorrah~~ *the Church* and how very grave their sin! Must I go down and see whether they have done altogether according to the outcry that has come to me?"

In the next chapter, we'll make a brief logical examination of the sins of Sodom and Gomorrah.

16. A Common Sense Examination of Genesis 19

When you compare what Genesis 19 says with the rest of the Bible, it cannot be concluded that Sodom's sin was same-sex desire. We can see further light by applying some logic and common sense to the passage.

If God destroyed the cities of the Plain because all of its inhabitants were homosexual, Samuel Kader indicates that

> out of the entire valley that encompasses Sodom as well as Gomorrah, *every person must be a homosexual*, every man, woman and child *minus nine individuals must be gay* if the city is being destroyed for that reason. This valley with all its surrounding cities must have ten heterosexuals to be spared, *if* the reason it is being destroyed is for homosexuality. (Kader 19)

However, the Lord doesn't tell Abraham the reason He is judging the cities is because their inhabitants are gay, but because their sin is "very grave" (Gen. 18:20). In his exchange with the Lord, it is *Abraham* who calls them "wicked" (18:23), as the writer of Genesis previously did in 13:13.

The Lord promises to spare if He can find ten *righteous* people there. What does it mean to be righteous? "What does Scripture say? 'Abraham *believed God*, and it was credited to him as righteousness'" (Rom. 4:3 NIV). Although Lot required some urging before he would act on the angels' message, he believed and obeyed.

Remember that *after* the angels struck blind the mob outside Lot's door, Lot ventured into the city to visit his sons-in-law-to-be: "Lot went out and warned the fiancés of his daughters, 'Evacuate this place; God is about to destroy this city!' But his daughters' would-be husbands treated it as a joke" (Gen. 19:14 MSG).

These young men, though *heterosexual*, did not believe Lot's message and therefore perished in the destruction as unrighteous. They did not believe Lot's warning—they rejected, as it were, the message of salvation. They thought Lot was jesting, but "it pleased God through the foolishness of the message preached to save those who believe" (1 Cor. 1:21 NKJV).

Genesis 19:4 states that "the people of Sodom, both young and old, *all the people*, from every quarter," gathered at Lot's door and demanded that the guests come out. Were they all gay?

Today San Francisco has the reputation for being the "gayest" city in the world. But even there, gay men make up far less than a quarter of the total male population. The gay, lesbian, and bisexual population of San Francisco is only 15.4% according to a 2006 study by the UCLA School of Law (Demographics). So, "to suggest that every man of every age in Sodom was homosexual is simply not credible" (Miner and Connoley 34).

Children are the offspring of heterosexual relationships. If all Sodom's men and women were homosexual, where did the children come from?

In this biblical account, something else is at work besides raw homosexual desire. If the men were gay and wanted only sex, it makes absolutely no sense for Lot to offer his daughters to them. The same applies to the Gibeah account in Judges 19. In offering his daughters, Lot must have known that the men outside were *predominantly heterosexual.*

What, then, is the explanation for the men of Sodom wanting to rape the visitors? Miner and Connoley have some cogent points to make:

> Consider an example from modern times. On August 9, 1997, in New York City, two white police officers were strip-searching a black Haitian immigrant named Abner Louima and grew angry with him. They dragged him into a bathroom and, while one officer held him down, the other repeatedly rammed a broken broom up Louima's rectum. While they did this, the officers reportedly yelled things like, "We're gonna teach you ni**ers to respect police officers." In the aftermath of this terrible incident, nobody has suggested the assault was motivated by homosexual desire. Intuitively, we recognize the two officers were motivated by hatred and fear of people like Abner Louima. *In their minds, there was no better way to demean and humiliate an "enemy" than to sexually violate him. ...*

They go on to explain:

> The motivation to sexually abuse those we hate is, sadly, part of the general human experience (even if it is not part of each of our personal experiences). *And it is this motivation, not homosexual desire, which stands behind the sin of Sodom.* Perhaps the men of that city feared the two angelic strangers

were spies. Perhaps the fact that Lot (a recent immigrant) had taken them in served to heighten their suspicion. Whatever caused their panic, a mob mentality took over, and before long the people of Sodom were at Lot's house clamoring to brutalize the strangers. *This is a story about attempted mob violence, not homosexual desire.* (Miner and Connoley 4–5, emphasis mine)

Second Peter 2:6 tells us that the Lord "condemned the cities of Sodom and Gomorrah by burning them to ashes and made them an example of what is going to happen to the *ungodly*" (NIV). *Ungodly* is asebeo, meaning "impious or wicked" (Strong's G764). The only other time this word appears (with other forms of it) is in Jude 15:

> [14]Enoch, the seventh from Adam, prophesied about them: "See, the Lord is coming with thousands upon thousands of his holy ones [15]to judge everyone, and to convict all of them of all the *ungodly* [asebeo] *acts* they have committed in their ungodliness, and of all the *defiant words* ungodly sinners have spoken against him." [16]These people are *grumblers and faultfinders*; they *follow their own evil desires*; they *boast about themselves* and *flatter others for their own advantage.*
>
> —JUDE 14–16 NIV

We see here that the ungodliness of verse 15 is described in verse 16: defiant words, speaking against the Lord, grumbling, faultfinding, following evil selfish desires, boasting, and flattering for self-advantage. God destroyed the cities of the Plain not for homosexuality, but for this kind of ungodliness and wickedness—all the sins listed in "Summary of the Biblical Sins of Sodom" on page 113.

One pointed question brings insight to the popular yet mistaken conclusion that the Genesis 19 passage condemns homosexuality:

If the two visitors had been WOMEN and the men of Sodom demanded to have sex with them, would we conclude that the purpose of the story was a blanket condemnation of HETEROSEXUALITY?

Of course not. Do we make that conclusion based on the Judges 19 passage where men rape a woman? No. Like medieval Church writers, we make no mention of it at all.

What is, then, the sin of Sodom?

The abomination of Sodom, according to the Old Testament prophets, was that they behaved with callous indifference toward the weak and vulnerable—the poor, orphans, widows, and strangers in their midst (Miner and Connoley 6).

Why does this make contemporary conservative believers uncomfortable? Matthew Vines offers an answer.

Christians often honor a hierarchy of sins. … [S]exual sins—especially when they are known publicly—are likely to be met with vocal opposition. This might begin to explain why it's difficult for some Christians to accept that the sin of Sodom had far more to do with a lack of hospitality and a bent toward violence than with any sexual designs the men had on Lot's visitors. (Vines 62–63)

As we have seen from a close study of the Scriptures, the sins of the cities of the Plain are arrogance and the violation of human rights that lead to inhospitality and brutal mistreatment of strangers. Despite how medieval Church writers twisted this understanding, God honors His Word and not religious opinions. The Bible alone suffices.

17. Historical Factors Contributing to the Misinterpretation

According to priest and psychotherapist John McNeill, the misinterpretation of the Sodom and Gomorrah narrative in Genesis 19 is perhaps the single most important factor in the Western Christian tradition condemning homosexuality.

For centuries the "Church taught, and people have universally believed... that homosexual practices had brought a terrible divine vengeance on the cities of Sodom and Gomorrah," and that when contemporary homosexual activity increased, it brought on God's wrath in the form of earthquakes, floods, famines, pestilence, and so on. Therefore, they had to ward off God's judgment by rooting out and punishing homosexuals (McNeill 42).

Much of the Church still believes that the sin which earned those ancient cities their destruction was "the habitual indulgence of perverse homosexual practices among men" (42). However, there is no evidence elsewhere in the Old Testament to show that homosexual behavior was prevalent in these cities.

"The Bible never identifies same-sex behavior as the sin of Sodom, or even as *a* sin of Sodom" (Vines 75), and "there is no text of the Christian Bible that determines the reading of Sodom as a story about same-sex copulation" (Jordan 32). "[T]he canonical treatment of [the Sodom and Gibeah] stories elsewhere in the Bible does not focus on the offense of male-male sex, but rather on violence and inhospitality" (Brownson 268–269).

> In spite of misleading English translations which may imply the contrary, *the word "homosexual" does not occur in the Bible*: no extant text or manuscript, Hebrew, Greek, Syriac, or Aramaic, contains such a word. In fact none of these languages ever contained a word corresponding to the English "homosexual," nor did any languages have such a term before the late nineteenth century. (Boswell 92)

Some believers may argue that the Bible condemns homosexuality elsewhere, as in Romans 1:18–32, 1 Corinthians 6:9, and 1 Timothy 1:10. But a careful examination combining Greek word study and historical context reveals that these passages, also, do not teach what modern believers think they teach. An in-depth analysis of these passages is found in *Bible, Gender, Sexuality* (William B. Eerdmans Publishing Co., 2013) by James V. Brownson, professor of New Testament at Western Theological Seminary, that the author highly recommends for study.

We must be careful to not impose modern notions upon ancient biblical texts; "it is anachronistic to imagine that the sexual preoccupations of later ages were major issues in such Old Testament stories as that of Sodom" (Boswell 96).

Hospitality primary in the Bible

The story of the destruction of Jericho in Joshua 6 is a testament to the importance of hospitality as compared to sexual offenses. Like Sodom, the Lord completely destroyed Jericho, saving only the family of Rahab—a prostitute—and prostitution is forbidden in Leviticus 19:29 and Deuteronomy 23:17.

Why was Rahab spared? Because she showed *hospitality* to the messengers of Joshua. "It was by faith that Rahab the prostitute was not destroyed with the people in her city who refused to obey God. *For she had given a friendly welcome to the spies*" (Heb. 11:31 NLT).

Remember what Origen wrote: "Hear these words, you who close your houses to strangers; hear these words, you who avoid a guest as an enemy.... *[Lot] escapes the conflagration for this reason alone: because he opened his house to strangers.* Angels entered the hospitable house; fire entered the houses closed to strangers" (Hom. Gen., emphasis mine).

> One must also bear in mind that such Old Testament writers were responding to the same story which some modern interpreters still claim "obviously" refer to "homosexuality" and that they were on a far more intimate footing than modern writers with both the language and life-style of the people involved. Their refusal to see the account as a moral about homosexual behavior cannot be lightly disregarded, especially in the face of so little evidence to support a homosexual interpretation. (Boswell 95)

Jewish commentaries primarily considered the sin of Sodom correctly as that of inhospitality. The gradual shift in belief that the sin of Sodom was homosexuality began in the early Christian era. Although the original biblical understanding of the sin of Sodom survived until the Middle Ages, "the increasing emphasis of Hellenistic Jewish and Christian moralists on sexual purity gave rise in late Jewish apocrypha and early Christian writings to associations of Sodom with sexual excesses of various sorts" (97).

The interpretation of the sin of Sodom as homosexuality developed over time and eventually took on a life of its own *not* based on sound examination and interpretation of the Scriptures.

The process of demonization

Mark D. Jordan traces this process throughout history, identifying the turning point as the propaganda of Damian's *Book of Gomorrah* (see "Peter Damian" on page 132). Damian coined the word *sodomy* as the result of a long process of "thinning and condensing."

The term *sodomite* was coined first by Amandus. The adjective *sodomitic* was first mentioned by Jerome. Adjectives must qualify something: "Most often in Christian theology it qualifies a sin or a crime, which is then blamed and analyzed, depicted and condemned" (Jordan 40–41). This process amounts to a religious broad-brushing that divorces original meaning and understanding from contemporary thought and treatment of a subject.

By the eighth century "Sodom and its inhabitants were being mentioned as a way of designating a particular kind of sexual intercourse." Some sections of penitential writings of that time "refer simply to 'Sodomites' as a class meriting a certain punishment." (41)

The complicated story of Sodom and its destruction was "simplified until it became the punishment of a single sin." This sin was transferred from the biblical understanding of pride, arrogance, cruelty, and inhospitality to the Roman category of *luxuria*—sins having to do with the genitals—and then narrowed to one particular sexual act. (29)

> The essential thing to notice in the processes by which [the term] "Sodomy" was produced is that they first abolish details, qualifications, restrictions in order to enable an excessive simplification in thought (29).

What are the implications of this process of abstraction from a historical name? "To abstract an essence from a proper name," in this case, *sodomite*, "is to reduce the person named to a single quality" (42). Abstraction allows writers to reduce their opponent to a "schematic caricature" (43).

This is the process of *demonization*.

We see this process at work in Jesus' day. The new disciple Phillip found Nathanael and told him about Jesus of Nazareth.

"Nazareth!" Nathanael exclaimed. "Can anything good come from there?"

Nazareth apparently had a reputation, and based on this widespread opinion, many people thought it impossible for anything good to come from there. "Nazareth" had been thinned and condensed and abstracted down to a single quality of worthlessness.

But what did Phillip answer? *"Come and see"* (Jn. 1:46 NIV). *Come*—exert some effort to overcome the inertia of opinion and stereotypes. *See*—open your eyes, look and examine for yourself. You might notice something new—the truth.

When God's people blindly accept religious or political opinion about a subject or a people and stop coming to see for themselves, they miss the revelation of Jesus. They become blind, like the citizens of Sodom.

When Jesus entered Jerusalem that final week, the crowds explained to the curious, "'This is Jesus, the prophet from Nazareth in Galilee'" (Mt. 21:11 NIV). Yet when the open-minded Nicodemus spoke of Jesus before the Pharisees, they responded according to the result of this blinding process:

> [50]Nicodemus, who had gone to Jesus earlier and who was one of their own number, asked, [51]"Does our law condemn a man without *first hearing him* to find out what he has been doing?"
> [52]They replied, "Are you from Galilee, too? *Look into it*, and you will find that a prophet does not come out of Galilee."
> —*JOHN 7:50–52 NIV*

The Pharisees spoke from a position they considered to be knowledge and understanding but which, in reality, was blindness and ignorance. They believed they knew the Scriptures yet—had they actually "looked into" the situation and discovered where Jesus was actually born (Bethlehem)—they would have kept themselves from error.

Demonization leads to blindness

This blinding happened to Saul of Tarsus on the road to Damascus.

In a self-righteous religious frenzy to stamp out those who were polluting the Hebrew religion and threatening the purity of the nation, Saul, "still breathing threats and murder against the disciples of the Lord" (Ac. 9:1), carries letters from the high priest to the synagogues of Damascus with plans to bind these "Christians" and bring them to Jerusalem.

> [3]Now as he was going along and approaching Damascus, suddenly *a light from heaven flashed around him.* [4]He fell to the ground and heard a voice saying to him, "Saul, Saul, why do you persecute me?"
>
> [5]He asked, "Who are you, Lord?"
>
> The reply came, "I am Jesus, whom you are persecuting. [6]But get up and enter the city, and you will be told what you are to do."
>
> [7]The men who were traveling with him stood speechless because they heard the voice but saw no one. [8]Saul got up from the ground, and *though his eyes were open, he could see nothing*; so they led him by the hand and brought him into Damascus. [9]For three days he was *without sight*, and neither ate nor drank.
>
> —ACTS 9:3–9

It is in this blindness of misguided religious zeal that God strikes Saul physically blind, effectively calling a halt to his sinful endeavors and, by removing a sense, brings him to his senses. By blinding him, Saul "sees the light."

In a vision (sanctified spiritual sight), the Lord speaks to Ananias and tells him that Saul "is an instrument whom I have chosen to bring my name before Gentiles and kings and before the people of Israel; I myself will show him how much he must suffer for the sake of my name" (vv. 15–16). Ananias obediently goes to Judas' house, lays his hands on Saul, and the Lord restores Saul's sight and fills him with the Holy Spirit (v. 17).

"And immediately something like scales fell from his eyes, and his sight was restored" (v. 18). *Scales* is the Greek word *lepis*, meaning "a flake, a scale" (Strong's G3013), and can refer to an eggshell, the skin of an onion, or a fish scale (Kittle, 4:232,529).

Through revelation and proper spiritual insight, blindness is removed, enabling Saul to see former enemies as friends—as well as a ministry field.

Another such a turnaround is demonstrated in the Old Testament attack of the Arameans. The King of Aram was at war with Israel and sent his army to surround the city of Dothan to capture the prophet Elisha.

Elisha's servant is disturbed upon seeing the encroaching enemy forces, but Elisha prays that *his eyes may be opened*, and the servant sees "the mountain was full of horses and chariots of fire all around" (2 Ki. 6:17). The presence of this angelic army lets Elisha know the battle is the Lord's.

> [18]When the Arameans came down against him, Elisha prayed to the Lord, and said, "Strike this people, please, with *blindness*." So he struck them with blindness as Elisha had asked. [19]Elisha said to them, "This is not the way, and this is not the city; follow me, and I will bring you to the man whom you seek." And he led them to Samaria.
> [20]As soon as they entered Samaria, Elisha said, "O Lord, open the eyes of these men so that they may see." *The Lord opened their eyes*, and they saw that they were inside Samaria.
> [21]When the king of Israel saw them he said to Elisha, "Father, shall I kill them? Shall I kill them?" [22]He answered, "No! Did you capture with your sword and your bow those whom you want to kill? *Set food and water before them so that they may*

eat and drink; and let them go to their master." ²³So *he prepared for them a great feast; after they ate and drank, he sent them on their way*, and they went to their master. And the Arameans no longer came raiding into the land of Israel.
—2 KINGS 6:18–23

Psalm 23 says, "You prepare a table before me in the presence of my enemies" (NKJV). "God does peacefully what man could only do possibly through acts of war" (Blinded). By bringing the enemy into the presence of the king and offering them *hospitality*, Elisha brings peace and unity to God's land. "[E]ating together under one roof constitutes a peace treaty in the Ancient Near East and Arameans would now be bound by social custom to not attack a friend who had extended a gift of hospitality" (Blinded).

Instead of destroying those formerly considered enemies, God's people accepted and obeyed the prophetic word to show them kindness (Lk. 6:35). Then they "let them go to their master," reminiscent of Jesus' words to the disciples, who sought to keep a certain class of people away: "Jesus said, 'Let the little children come to me, and do not stop them; for it is to such as these that the kingdom of heaven belongs'" (Mt. 19:14).

But in the medieval Church, the Pharisaical and Saulish blinding process took hold with the polluting polemic of Peter Damian.

That transition from acts to persons is perhaps what an essence does best. By coining an abstract term to group together a series of acts, Peter Damian has made the inference from acts to agent almost automatic. The acts display an essence, the essence of Sodomy. … [Sodomites] are no longer persons who perform a few similar acts from a myriad of motives and in incalculably different circumstances. They are Sodomites doing Sodomy. The abstractive power of the word abolishes motives and circumstances. (Jordan 44)

You can see this process powerfully at work in today's socio-political scene. The world still struggles over LGBT rights, racial issues, immigration, other religions. The world still broad-brushes outsiders with terms like *foreigner, sinner, liberal, queer.* "The term 'Sodomy' makes possible a number of theological descriptions in which the realities of human lives are lied about, are deliberately misrepresented, for allegedly moral purposes" (Jordan 164). It is even more unfortunate that much of this narrow-mindedness and persecution have come from the Church.

Because of the Church's long-standing mistreatment of others, the term *Christian* is being abstracted to mean one who is ignorant of the facts, unversed in their own Scriptures, bigoted and prejudiced against those unlike themselves religiously and politically, and demonizing and cruel to gays, lesbians, and trans people. When this process runs full course, all Christians may be categorized and treated in the way they have handled the LGBT community and individuals for the past millennium.

In the years leading up to the publication of this book, hostility also has grown among U.S. political conservatives (many of which are evangelicals) towards unwed mothers, wage-class workers, the poor, immigrants, and Muslims. This should concern followers of Christ because it is the path that Sodom took toward those they perceived as outsiders. When we consider the reasons for the Lord's response to the cities of the Plain, it should cause us to examine our own hearts and stand against intolerance and inhospitableness not only in the Church but greater society, lest God visit our nation with judgment.

God is not mocked. Whatever the Church sows, that will it also reap (Gal. 6:7-8). Perhaps you have not participated personally in this mistreatment of others. But the Church must police its own lest it be judged by the actions of its most misinformed members.[49]

Realizing our mistakes and properly understanding the Scriptures and the errors of Church history must lead to repentance.

---

49 See Luke 6:37; 1 Corinthians 6:1-5; 1 Peter 4:17.

18. Conclusion and Challenge

We see from a study of the Scriptures—*all* the passages which mention Sodom—that the sins of the cities of the Plain are idolatry, pride, gluttony, violence, hatred of strangers, and inhospitality to outsiders, not same-sex coupling.

When we compare Genesis 19 with the Judges 19 account of Gibeah, we understand that rape, "the dehumanization of one human being by another" (Horner 48), is the ultimate expression of their hostility and violence toward strangers, whether male or female.

Study of Scriptures should suffice to determine what the sin of Sodom was. This is especially true when we use the Bible to form doctrine about Christian living with the danger of condemning entire classes of people.

Christian teaching should speak only as the Scriptures teach. It should conform its logic and argument to that of the Scriptures. Most important, it should remain silent when the Scriptures are silent. Jordan asks:

> Do we meet these tests when we invoke the history of Christian moral teaching to speak about what we call homosexuality? Our readings in medieval texts have suggested that we do not meet them. Indeed, we fail much lesser tests. We typically disregard the most basic rules of respectful reading when arguing about same-sex love. We rip words out of context; we

magnify what is microscopic and ignore what is enormous; we refuse to examine the rifts that divide our languages, our discourses, from the patristic or medieval discourses we want to invoke. (Jordan 160)

The Apostle Peter admitted some things in Scripture are hard to understand, "which untaught and unstable people twist to their own destruction, as they do also the rest of the Scriptures" (2Pet. 3:16b NKJV). But we must be diligent to correctly interpret and apply its teachings.

This wrenching of the Scriptures leads to the abstracting process of demonization.

The procedures of abstraction are what make the term "Sodomy" so unstable. It contains within itself a mistaken reading and a mistaken way of inferring moral truths. ... It pretends to speak a lesson from Genesis 19. In fact, it misreads that chapter allegorically and then illicitly generalizes from allegory to lawlike definition and prescription. (162–163)

The crimes of the destroyed ancient cities changed from the original understanding to focus solely on one type of sexual behavior. From there, the term *sodomy* was coined and abstracted to refer to homosexual behavior and then to homosexuality in general.[50]

"There are two separate mistakes here" Jordan points out. "The first is to think that the story of Sodom is centrally about same-sex pleasure—or even a particular kind of same-sex copulation. It is not" (162). Yet, a great segment of the Church believes that all homosexuals are *sodomites*, worthy of a fiery death sentence.

The citizens of Sodom lumped together all outsiders as strangers, suspicious as a class and worthy to be abused and violated. They reduced travelers to certain victimhood in every case. Just as nothing good could come from Nazareth, nothing good could come from outside the walls of Sodom. Horner discusses this process of demonization:

> It is doubly unfortunate that a great portion of the public identifies all homosexuality with the conduct of the men of Sodom and says, "The men of Sodom were bad; therefore all homosexuality is bad." Well, the men of Sodom *were* bad, but they were bad not because of their homosexuality but because they had allowed themselves to become so callous in their dealings with other human beings that they had turned themselves into brutes. (Horner 47)

Those who name Jesus Christ as their Savior and claim to live according to the Bible must see that such disregard and mistreatment of people, even if they're considered "sinners," is unquestionably unchristian and bring reproach upon not only the Gospel message, but the Lord himself.

---

50 "The last thing we should do is to translate 'Sodomy' as 'homosexuality.' 'Homosexuality' is a term from late nineteenth-century forensic medicine, a diagnostic term for regulating the behavior of the patients or prisoners it presumes to classify. If you ask, What does medieval moral theology have to say about homosexuality? the only precise answer is, absolutely nothing. 'Homosexuality' is no more discussed by medieval theology than are phlogiston, Newton's inertia, quarks or any of the other entities hypothesized by one or another modern science. 'Sodomy' is not 'homosexuality'" (Jordan 161).

When we, in our own relationships, disregard other human beings as persons we kill them little by little. It is ironic that for almost two thousand years in Western culture this is how those have been treated who have been honest enough with themselves to accept homosexuality as a (given) fact of their existence. They have been treated as less than human for no other reason than that they have expressed a sexual preference for members of their own sex.

If we would begin to judge people as individual persons, instead of prejudging them on the basis of their sexual preference, maybe we would begin to see where the real propensity for violence and lawbreaking in our society lies. (Horner 57)

McNeill aptly states an irony: for 1000 years in the Christian West, homosexuals have been the recipients of inhospitable treatment. "Condemned by the Church, they have been the victims of persecution, torture, and even death" (McNeill 42).

There is a sad irony about the story of Sodom when understood in its own historical setting. People oppose and abuse homosexual men and women for being different, odd, strange or, as they say, "queer." Lesbian women and gay men are just not allowed to fit in. They are made to be outsiders, foreigners in our society. They are disowned by their families, separated from their children, fired from their jobs, evicted from apartments and neighborhoods, insulted by public figures, denounced from the pulpit, vilified on religious radio and TV, and then beaten in the schools and killed on the streets and in the backwoods of our nation. All this is done in the name of religion and supposed Judeo-Christian morality.

Such wickedness is the very sin of which the people of Sodom were guilty. Such cruelty is what the Bible truly condemns over and over again. So those who oppress homosexuals because of the supposed "sin of Sodom" may themselves be the real "sodomites," as the Bible understands it. (Helminiak 49–50, emphasis mine)

In some parts of the Church, there is neither mercy nor forgiveness for those who identify themselves as homosexual. "Sodomy," says Jordan, "seems to be an unrepentable sin—that is, either an exception to divine grace or not a sin at all" (Jordan 162).[51]

Yet God's promise to those who are hospitable to strangers, those who accept the outsider and the Gospel messenger remains:

> I will restore their fortunes, the fortunes of Sodom and her daughters and the fortunes of Samaria and her daughters, and I will restore your own fortunes along with theirs...
> —*EZEKIEL 16:53*

Two final questions:

- What will you do to combat the ignorance and misinformation of the Church?
- How will you treat the stranger in our midst?

The Judge of All the Earth is awaits your answer. Jesus said, "Repent, for the kingdom of heaven is at hand."

---

51 There is only one unrepentable sin, blasphemy against the Holy Spirit (Mk. 3:29; Lk 12:10).

Appendix A: Genesis 18–19 NRSV

The following are chapters 18 and 19 of Genesis from the New Revised Standard Version. (*New Revised Standard Version Bible*, copyright © 1989 the Division of Christian Education of the National Council of the Churches of Christ in the United States of America. Used by permission.)

Chapter 18

¹The Lord appeared to Abraham by the oaks of Mamre, as he sat at the entrance of his tent in the heat of the day. ²He looked up and saw three men standing near him. When he saw them, he ran from the tent entrance to meet them, and bowed down to the ground. ³He said, "My lord, if I find favor with you, do not pass by your servant. ⁴Let a little water be brought, and wash your feet, and rest yourselves under the tree. ⁵Let me bring a little bread, that you may refresh yourselves, and after that you may pass on—since you have come to your servant." So they said, "Do as you have said." ⁶And Abraham hastened into the tent to Sarah, and said, "Make ready quickly three measures of choice flour, knead it, and make cakes." ⁷Abraham ran to the herd, and took a calf, tender and good, and gave it to the servant, who hastened to prepare it. ⁸Then he took curds and milk and the calf that he had prepared, and set it before them; and he stood by them under the tree while they ate.

⁹They said to him, "Where is your wife Sarah?" And he said, "There, in the tent." ¹⁰Then one said, "I will surely return to you in due season, and your wife Sarah shall have a son." And Sarah was listening at the tent entrance behind him. ¹¹Now Abraham and Sarah were old, advanced in age; it had ceased to be with Sarah after the manner of women. ¹²So Sarah laughed to herself, saying, "After I have grown old, and my husband is old, shall I have pleasure?" ¹³The Lord said to Abraham, "Why did Sarah laugh, and say, 'Shall I indeed bear a child, now that I am old?' ¹⁴Is anything too wonderful for the Lord? At the set time I will return to you, in due season, and Sarah shall have a son." ¹⁵But Sarah denied, saying, "I did not laugh"; for she was afraid. He said, "Oh yes, you did laugh."

¹⁶Then the men set out from there, and they looked toward Sodom; and Abraham went with them to set them on their way. ¹⁷The Lord said, "Shall I hide from Abraham what I am about to do, ¹⁸seeing that Abraham shall become a great and mighty nation, and all the nations of the earth shall be blessed in him? ¹⁹No, for I have chosen him, that he may charge his children and his household after him to keep the way of the Lord by doing righteousness and justice; so that the Lord may bring about for Abraham what he has promised him." ²⁰Then the Lord said, "How great is the outcry against Sodom and Gomorrah and how very grave their sin! ²¹I must go down and see whether they have done altogether according to the outcry that has come to me; and if not, I will know."

²²So the men turned from there, and went toward Sodom, while Abraham remained standing before the Lord. ²³Then Abraham came near and said, "Will you indeed sweep away the righteous with the wicked? ²⁴Suppose there are fifty

righteous within the city; will you then sweep away the place and not forgive it for the fifty righteous who are in it? 25Far be it from you to do such a thing, to slay the righteous with the wicked, so that the righteous fare as the wicked! Far be that from you! Shall not the Judge of all the earth do what is just?" 26And the Lord said, "If I find at Sodom fifty righteous in the city, I will forgive the whole place for their sake." 27Abraham answered, "Let me take it upon myself to speak to the Lord, I who am but dust and ashes. 28Suppose five of the fifty righteous are lacking? Will you destroy the whole city for lack of five?" And he said, "I will not destroy it if I find forty-five there." 29Again he spoke to him, "Suppose forty are found there." He answered, "For the sake of forty I will not do it." 30Then he said, "Oh do not let the Lord be angry if I speak. Suppose thirty are found there." He answered, "I will not do it, if I find thirty there." 31He said, "Let me take it upon myself to speak to the Lord. Suppose twenty are found there." He answered, "For the sake of twenty I will not destroy it." 32Then he said, "Oh do not let the Lord be angry if I speak just once more. Suppose ten are found there." He answered, "For the sake of ten I will not destroy it." 33And the Lord went his way, when he had finished speaking to Abraham; and Abraham returned to his place.

Chapter 19

1The two angels came to Sodom in the evening, and Lot was sitting in the gateway of Sodom. When Lot saw them, he rose to meet them, and bowed down with his face to the ground. 2He said, "Please, my lords, turn aside to your servant's house and spend the night, and wash your feet; then you can rise early and go on your way." They said, "No; we will spend the night in the square." ³But he urged them strongly; so they turned aside to him and entered his house; and he made them a feast, and baked unleavened bread, and they ate. ⁴But before they lay down, the men of the city, the men of Sodom, both young and old, all the people to the last man, surrounded the house; ⁵and they called to Lot, "Where are the men who came to you tonight? Bring them out to us, so that we may know them." ⁶Lot went out of the door to the men, shut the door after him, ⁷and said, "I beg you, my brothers, do not act so wickedly. ⁸Look, I have two daughters who have not known a man; let me bring them out to you, and do to them as you please; only do nothing to these men, for they have come under the shelter of my roof." ⁹But they replied, "Stand back!" And they said, "This fellow came here as an alien, and he would play the judge! Now we will deal worse with you than with them." Then they pressed hard against the man Lot, and came near the door to break it down. ¹⁰But the men inside reached out their hands and brought Lot into the house with them, and shut the door. ¹¹And they struck with blindness the men who were at the door of the house, both small and great, so that they were unable to find the door.

¹²Then the men said to Lot, "Have you anyone else here? Sons-in-law, sons, daughters, or anyone you have in the city— bring them out of the place. ¹³For we are about to destroy this place, because the outcry against its people has become great before the Lord, and the Lord has sent us to destroy it." ¹⁴So Lot went out and said to his sons-in-law, who were to marry his daughters, "Up, get out of this place; for the Lord is about to destroy the city." But he seemed to his sons-in-law to be jesting.

[15]When morning dawned, the angels urged Lot, saying, "Get up, take your wife and your two daughters who are here, or else you will be consumed in the punishment of the city." [16]But he lingered; so the men seized him and his wife and his two daughters by the hand, the Lord being merciful to him, and they brought him out and left him outside the city. [17]When they had brought them outside, they said, "Flee for your life; do not look back or stop anywhere in the Plain; flee to the hills, or else you will be consumed." [18]And Lot said to them, "Oh, no, my lords; [19]your servant has found favor with you, and you have shown me great kindness in saving my life; but I cannot flee to the hills, for fear the disaster will overtake me and I die. [20]Look, that city is near enough to flee to, and it is a little one. Let me escape there—is it not a little one?—and my life will be saved!" [21]He said to him, "Very well, I grant you this favor too, and will not overthrow the city of which you have spoken. [22]Hurry, escape there, for I can do nothing until you arrive there." Therefore the city was called Zoar. [23]The sun had risen on the earth when Lot came to Zoar.

[24]Then the Lord rained on Sodom and Gomorrah sulfur and fire from the Lord out of heaven; [25]and he overthrew those cities, and all the Plain, and all the inhabitants of the cities, and what grew on the ground. [26]But Lot's wife, behind him, looked back, and she became a pillar of salt.

[27]Abraham went early in the morning to the place where he had stood before the Lord; [28]and he looked down toward Sodom and Gomorrah and toward all the land of the Plain and saw the smoke of the land going up like the smoke of a furnace.

[29]So it was that, when God destroyed the cities of the Plain, God remembered Abraham, and sent Lot out of the midst of the overthrow, when he overthrew the cities in which Lot had settled.

[30]Now Lot went up out of Zoar and settled in the hills with his two daughters, for he was afraid to stay in Zoar; so he lived in a cave with his two daughters. [31]And the firstborn said to the younger, "Our father is old, and there is not a man on earth to come in to us after the manner of all the world. [32]Come, let us make our father drink wine, and we will lie with him, so that we may preserve offspring through our father." [33]So they made their father drink wine that night; and the firstborn went in, and lay with her father; he did not know when she lay down or when she rose. [34]On the next day, the firstborn said to the younger, "Look, I lay last night with my father; let us make him drink wine tonight also; then you go in and lie with him, so that we may preserve offspring through our father." [35]So they made their father drink wine that night also; and the younger rose, and lay with him; and he did not know when she lay down or when she rose. [36]Thus both the daughters of Lot became pregnant by their father. [37]The firstborn bore a son, and named him Moab; he is the ancestor of the Moabites to this day. [38]The younger also bore a son and named him Ben-ammi; he is the ancestor of the Ammonites to this day.

Appendix B: Peoples of Genesis 14:5–7

The following are descriptions of the peoples listed in Genesis 14:5–7 and their territories.

Rephaim in Ashteroth-karnaim

The Rephaim were a race of giants, perhaps the offspring between human women and fallen angels (Gen. 6:4; Jude 6). *Rephaim* means "giants" and comes from a base word meaning "to sink down or be disheartened" (Harris, Archer and Waltke, 2198d). This was the effect of Goliath upon the soldiers of Israel in King Saul's day (see 1 Sam. 17:11).

Ashteroth-karnaim was a northern city in the territory of Bashan, east of the Sea of Chinnereth, later known as Lake Gennesaret and then the Sea of Galilee (May 57, 77, 85). "The name translates literally to 'Ashteroth of the Horns', with 'Ashteroth' being a Canaanite fertility goddess and 'horns' being symbolic of mountain peaks" (Ashteroth Karnaim). It was the seat of worship for the goddess (Packer, Tenney and White 685).

Zuzim in Ham

The *Zuzim*, meaning "restless or roaming" (Zuzim, biblical people), were an aboriginal tribe of Palestine (Strong's H2104).

Ham was a city that lay east of the Jordan (May 57), between Astheroth-karnaim and Moabite country (Packer, Tenney and White 702).

"Many scholars identify the Zuzim with the Zamzummim (Deuteronomy 2:20), a tribe of the Rephaim living in the same region as the Zuzim and later occupied by the Ammonites. In Hebrew 'Zuz' represents the root 'z'z' which means, 'to move'" (Zuzim, biblical people). The Zuzim were apparently a primitive nomadic nation and could also be one of the races of giants.

Emim in Shaveh-kiriathaim

Emim means "terrors" (Strong's H368) or "the dreaded ones" (Emite). Deuteronomy 2:10–11 explains, "The Emim had dwelt there in times past, a people as great and numerous and tall as the Anakim. *They were also regarded as giants*, like the Anakim, but the Moabites call them Emim" (NKJV).

Shaveh-kiriathaim means "the plains of Kiriathaim" (Packer, Tenney and White 725) and indicates a double city (Strong's H7741), lying just east of the Salt Sea (May 57). "The strength of these cities engendered 'the pride' of Moab (Isa. 16:6)" (Jamieson, Fausset and Brown Eze. 25:9, Kiriathaim).

Later, Jeremiah prophesied that Kiriathaim in Moab would be put to shame and taken captive, and that judgment would come upon it (Jer. 48:1,23 HCSB).

Horites in Seir as far as El-paran

Horites comes from a word that means "cavedweller, troglodyte" (Strong's H2752).

"Mt. Seir seems to have been named after one Seir, who… 'the land of Seir' was [also] named after (Genesis 14:6). He was the ancestor of the Horite chiefs" listed in Genesis 36:20–30 (Horites). The Horites later "co-existed and inter-married with the family of Esau, grandson of Abraham through Isaac (Genesis 25:21–25)" (Horites).

El-Paran means "oak of Paran" (Strong's H364); *Paran* means "ornamental" (Strong's H6290) or "beautiful" (Packer, Tenney and White 719). Paran was "a wilderness seven days' march from Mount Sinai (Gen. 21:21; Num. 10:12; 1 Sam. 25:1)" (719). It is a "district or area in the northeast section of the Sinai peninsula, southwest of Edom, and south of the wilderness of Zin near the Judean mountains" (Harris, Archer and Waltke, 1728). This is quite far south of all the other territories—between the Gulf of Suez and the Gulf of Aqaba north of the Red Sea (May 59).

Enmishpat, Kadesh

Enmishpat means "fountain of judgment" (Strong's H5880). *Kadesh* means "sanctuary" (Strong's H6946). Kadesh is about 50 miles southwest of the southern end of the Salt Sea.

Amalekites

Although Amalek had not yet been born (Amalek is a descendant of Esau, the son of Eliphaz and the concubine Timna: Gen. 36:12; 1 Chr. 1:36), the writer of Genesis refers to the territory that the descendants of Amalek later possessed.

"The center of this Amalekite territory was North of Kadesh-barnea in the Negev desert in the southern part of Palestine, with their tributary camps radiating out into the Sinai Peninsula and northern Arabia (1 Sam. 15:7)" (Amalek). It lay between Kadesh and the southwestern tip of the Salt Sea.

Amorites in Hazazon-tamar

Amorites comes from words meaning "publicity" or "moun-taineer" (Strong H567). The Amorites were located west of the Salt Sea and lived in the mountains. "In the third millennium B.C. the Amorite kingdom spread over the greater part of Mesopotamia and Syria-Palestine, the latter being designated as the 'land of the Amorites'" (Harris, Archer and Waltke, 119).

Hazazon-tamar means "sandy surface of the palm tree" (Packer, Tenney and White 704). It is the ancient name of En-gedi in Syria (Dake). It is about twenty miles southwest of the Dead Sea (May 59).

Works Cited

"Amalek." 08 June 2015. *Wikipedia.org*. Web. 09 July 2015. <https://en.wikipedia.org/wiki/Amalek>.

"Ashteroth Karnaim." 28 Feb. 2013. *Wikipedia.org*. Web. 09 July 2015. <https://en.wikipedia.org/wiki/Ashteroth_Karnaim>.

"Bible Names." n.d. *Bible History Online (Bible-history.com)*. Web. 06 July 2015. <http://www.bible-history.com/links.php?cat=43&sub=1070&cat_name=Bible+Names>.

"Blinded By The Light: Being Struck Blind in Scripture." Aug. 2013. *Souljournaler.blogspot.com*. Web. 31 Aug. 2015. <http://souljournaler.blogspot.com/2013/08/blinded-by-light-being-struck-blind-in.html>.

Boswell, John. *Christianity, Social Tolerance, and Homosexuality*. Chicago, IL: University of Chicago Press, 1980. Print.

Brownson, James V. *Bible, Gender, Sexuality: Reframing the Church's Debate on Same-Sex Relationships*. Grand Rapids, MI: William B. Eerdmans Publishing Company, 2013. Print.

"Calotropis procera." 19 July 2015. *Wikipedia.org*. Web. 24 Aug. 2015. <https://en.wikipedia.org/wiki/Calotropis_procera>.

Calvin, John. "Commentary on Genesis, vol. 1." 13 July 2005. *Christian Classics Ethereal Library*. Web. 18 July 2015. <http://www.ccel.org/ccel/calvin/calcom01.xxiv.i.html>.

Carden, Michael. *Sodomy: A History of a Christian Biblical Myth.* London, UK: Equinox Publishing Ltd., 2004. Print.

Chandler, Paul-Gordon. "Sacred Hospitality 'Middle Eastern Style'." December 2005. *PaulGordonChandler.com.* Web (PDF). 02 July 2015. <http://temp.paulgordonchandler.com/wp-content/uploads/2013/01/Sacred-Hospitality-Middle-Eastern-Style-Inland-Episcopalian.pdf>.

Dake, Finis J. *Dake's Annotated Reference Bible.* Lawrenceville, GA: Dake Bible Sales, Inc., 1997. WORDsearch CROSS e-book.

"Demographics of Sexual Orientation." 01 July 2015. *Wikipedia.org.* Web. 02 July 2015. <https://en.wikipedia.org/wiki/Demographics_of_sexual_orientation>.

Easton, Matthew George. *Illustrated Bible Dictionary: And Treasury of Biblical History, Biography, Geography, Doctrine, and Literature.* London, UK: T. Nelson and Sons, 1897. WORDsearch CROSS e-book.

"Elam." 01 July 2015. *Wikipedia.org.* Web. 05 July 2015. <https://en.wikipedia.org/wiki/Elam>.

"Emite." 25 Apr. 2015. *Wikipedia.org.* Web. 09 July 2015. <https://en.wikipedia.org/wiki/Emite>.

"Gutian people." 09 June 2015. *Wikipedia.org.* Web. 06 July 2015. <https://en.wikipedia.org/wiki/Gutian_people>.

Harris, R. Laird, Gleason L. Archer and Bruce K. Waltke, *Theological Wordbook of the Old Testament.* Chicago, IL, 1980. WORDsearch CROSS e-book.

Helminiak, Daniel A. *What the Bible Really Says About Homosexuality*. New Mexico: Alamo Square Press, 2000. Print.

"Horites." 18 Apr. 2015. *Wikipedia.org*. Web. 09 July 2015. <https://en.wikipedia.org/wiki/Horites>.

Horner, Tom. *Jonathan Loved David: Homosexuality in Biblical Times*. Philadelphia, PA: Westminster Press, 1978. Print.

Jacobs, Joseph and Schulim Ochser. "Sodom." 1906. *JewishEncylopedia.com*. Web. 25 Aug. 2015. <http://www.jewishencyclopedia.com/articles/13827-sodom>.

Jamieson, Robert, A.R. Fausset and David Brown. *Commentary: Critical, Experimental, and Practical on the Old and New Testaments, A*. Toledo, OH, 1884. WORDsearch CROSS e-book.

Jordan, Mark D. *Invention of Sodomy in Christian Theology, The*. Chicago, IL: The University of Chicago Press, 1997. Print.

Josephus, Flavius. *Works of Josephus: New and Updated Edition, The*. Trans. William Whiston. Peabody, MA: Hendrickson Publishers, 1987. Print.

Kader, Samuel. *Openly Gay, Openly Christian: How the Bible Really Is Gay Friendly*. Grapevine, TX: SEGR Publishing LLC, 2013. Print.

Kittle, Gerhard, ed. *Theological Dictionary of the New Testament*. Trans. Goeffrey W. Bromiley. Grand Rapids, MI: William B. Eerdmans Publishing Company, 1964. WORDsearch CROSS e-book.

Lightfoot, John. "The Sea of Sodom." 1658. *Biblehub.com*. Web. 25 Aug. 2015. <http://biblehub.com/library/lightfoot/

from_the_talmud_and_hebraica/
chapter_5_the_sea_of.htm>.

Loader, James Alfred. *Tale of Two Cities: Sodom and Gomorrah in the Old Testament, Early Jewish and Early Christian Traditions.* Leuven, Belgium: Peeters Publishers, 1990. Print.

May, Herbert G., ed. *Oxford Bible Atlas.* 2nd ed. London, UK: Oxford University Press, 1974. Print.

McNeill, John. *Church and the Homosexual, The.* 4th ed. Boston, MA: Beacon Press, 1993. Print.

Miller, Madeleine S. and J. Lane. *Harper's Bible Dictionary.* New York, NY: Harper & Brothers, Publishers, 1954. Print.

Miner, Jeff and John Tyler Connoley. *Children Are Free, The.* Indianapolis, IN: Jesus Metropolitan Community Church, 2002. Print.

NIV Study Bible. Grand Rapids, MI: Zondervan Corporation, 1985. Print.

Packer, J. I., Merrill C. Tenney and William White, *Bible Almanac, The.* Nashville, TN: Thomas Nelson Publishers, 1980. Print.

"Pat Robertson controversies." 03 May 2015. *Wikipedia.org.* Web. 02 July 2015. <https://en.wikipedia.org/wiki/Pat_Robertson_controversies>.

Philo. "On Abraham." ca. 30. *Well.com.* Web. 27 Aug. 2015. <http://www.well.com/~aquarius/philo-abraham.htm>.

Rotherham, Joseph Bryant. *Emphasized Bible.* Grand Rapids, MI: Kregel Publications, 1994. Print.

"Sin (mythology)." 16 June 2015. *Wikipedia.org.* Web. 03 July 2015. <https://en.wikipedia.org/wiki/ Sin_%28mythology%29>.

Smith, William. *Smith's Bible Dictionary: Comprising Antiquities, Biography, Geography, Natural History, Archaeology and Literature.* Philadelphia, PA: A.J. Holman & Co., 1901. WORDsearch CROSS e-book.

"Sodom and Gomorrah." 27 June 2015. *Wikipedia.org.* Web. 02 July 2015. <https://en.wikipedia.org/wiki/ Sodom_and_Gomorrah>.

Strong, James. *Strong's Talking Greek & Hebrew Dictionary.* Austin, TX, 2007. WORDsearch CROSS e-book.

"Talmud." 20 Aug. 2015. *Wikipedia.org.* Web. 27 Aug. 2015. <https://en.wikipedia.org/wiki/Talmud>.

"Tidal (Bible)." 08 Apr. 2015. *Wikipedia.org.* Web. 06 July 2015. <https://en.wikipedia.org/wiki/Tidal_%28Bible%29>.

"Ur." 15 June 2015. *Wikipedia.org.* Web. 03 July 2015. <https:// en.wikipedia.org/wiki/Ur>.

"Ur Kasdim." 16 June 2015. *Wikipedia.org.* Web. 03 July 2015. <https://en.wikipedia.org/wiki/Ur_Ka%C5%9Bdim>.

"Vine of Sodom." 06 June 2015. *Wikipedia.org.* Web. 24 Aug. 2015. <https://en.wikipedia.org/wiki/Vine_of_Sodom>.

Vines, Matthew. *God and the Gay Christian: The Biblical Case in Support of Same-Sex Relationships.* New York, NY: Convergent Books, 2014. Print.

Wood, Bryant G. "Discovery of the Sin Cities of Sodom and Gomorrah, The." 16 Apr. 2008. *Associates for Biblical*

Research (biblearchaeology.org). Web. 05 July 2015. <http://www.biblearchaeology.org/post/2008/04/The-Discovery-of-the-Sin-Cities-of-Sodom-and-Gomorrah.aspx>.

"Zoara." 13 June 2015. *Wikipedia.org.* Web. 06 July 2015. <https://en.wikipedia.org/wiki/Zoara>.

"Zuzim, biblical people." 02 Feb. 2014. *Wikipedia.org.* Web. 09 July 2015. <https://en.wikipedia.org/wiki/Zuzim_%28biblical_people%29>.

www.ingramcontent.com/pod-product-compliance
Lightning Source LLC
Chambersburg PA
CBHW020906100426
42737CB00044B/385